TIGER MOM YOUR CHILD TO NOT ONLY BE SUCCESSFUL BUT DOMINATE

By Katherine Shepard

Table of Contents

CHAPTER ONE: INTRODUCTION

The different ways that folks shape their youngsters' advancement have been a customary wellspring of estimating by researchers, thinkers and, middle of everyone's attention, by folks themselves. Inside of the scientific point of view, a significant part of the observational work connecting parental conduct to formative results in kids has been delivered by those working in brain research, social science and criminology. In any case, different orders have contributed both speculations and strategies including history specialists, anthropologists also, organic sciences. Case in point, findings from ethnology have illustrated the organic premise and developmental significance of the kid's connection to the guardian, while explore in physiology, endocrinology and hereditary qualities has influenced impressively our comprehension of child rearing and its consequences for posterity.

In any case, there are additionally all the more squeezing and reasonable inspirations driving current enthusiasm for this point. Boss among these is developing worry about the sizeable and maybe developing extent of kids with generous instructive, social and wellbeing issues, combined with a conviction that changing the family environment may be a strong method for enhancing kids' lives and life shots. Structure and extent of this survey we open with a brief survey of the verifiable and contemporary connections in which child rearing and child rearing exploration were and are seen. We then diagram some of the significant hypotheses and models that overwhelm examine on parent–child connections furthermore, tyke results. The third part audits center methodological contemplations to analyze the connection between how data is acquired and what findings are produced from it. We go ahead to consider the general ability of the exploration findings, including the degree to which social and sub cultural requirements confine the materialness of findings. It is in this connection that we likewise consider child rearing as a 'general wellbeing' concern, and the degree to which current strategy patterns are receptive to the effect of child rearing in the wellbeing and prosperity of the country. At long last, we consider specific favorable circumstances, concerns and headings for further research. Examination demonstrates that the vast majority think strict child rearing delivers better-carried on children. Be that as it may, inquire about studies on order reliably demonstrate that strict, or tyrant, kid bringing up really delivers kids with lower self regard who carry on more awful than different children - and consequently get rebuffed more! Strict child rearing really makes conduct issues in kids. Why?

From the streets to success: How I conceived the need of Strict Parenting

The thought that people have rights springs from the weakness of each person despite more grounded strengths. Our Declaration of Independence and Constitution are in light of the thought that the motivation behind government is not to secure the world class, nor to encourage avarice or self-interest nor to advance a religious bunch's plan. Its design is to ensure certain natural human rights for all individuals including our country's successors... our young natives.

The greater part of us assumes that parents have rights that give them restrictive control over their children, particularly infants. Yet, the need to indicate those rights just emerges when things turn out badly in families and in child-serving organizations. Sadly, the sincerely charged issue of parental rights emerges all the time today. Parents force state intercession when they disregard and misuse or question authority of their children. Minors conceive an offspring. An excess of child-serving establishments are overburdened and not able to capacity adequately.

Notwithstanding characterizing who is a guardian can be confounded. With surrogate conception and manual sperm injection, characterizing a mother and a father can be entangled. By dispensing with the equivocal term "normal guardian" from its standards for building up a lawful guardian child relationship, the Uniform Parentage Act urges courts to concentrate on the exact relationship a female or male has to a child. Is the relationship of every mother and father: 1) hereditary, 2) conception (mother just), 3) useful, 4) stepparent, or 5) supportive? A solitary child could have upwards of nine distinct persons lawfully perceived as a guardian by including 6) cultivate, 7) stage, 8) surrogate and 9) sperm or egg benefactor.

Parental Rights

In view of their commitments to their children, parents need rights or privileges to ensure and satisfy the human privileges of their children. Sadly, contemporary discuss human rights ordinarily underscores the rights to advantages and disregards the obligations that go with those rights.

Previously, children have been dealt with as the individual property of their parents. Under Roman law, the patria protestas tenet gave fathers life and passing control over their children. Right up 'til the present time, the prominent assumption is that children have a place with their parents.

Conversely, since The Enlightenment of the Eighteenth Century, parenthood in Western societies has been seen as an agreement in the middle of parents and society by thinkers and developing legitimate codes. Parents are honored rights in return for releasing their obligations.

John Locke in the Seventeenth Century and William Blackstone in the Eighteenth Century held that parental rights and forces emerge from their obligation to administer to their posterity. They perceived that no general public can survive unless its children grow up to be capable, gainful residents. Children likewise have the privilege to be raised without unjustified impedance by the state. Taken together, these rights are known as the privilege of family uprightness. Both Locke and Blackstone held that, if a decision is constrained upon society, it is more critical to secure the privileges of children than to ensure the privileges of grown-ups.

Each man and each lady has a characteristic and Constitutional right to reproduce. This rule could be sensibly connected when the onset of menarche was somewhere around sixteen and eighteen. Since menarche shows up overall at twelve years old, we must inquire as to whether each young lady and kid has a characteristic and Constitutional right to multiply. In the light of this question, the requirement for cautious contemplated parental rights and obligations is increased.

The Child-Parent Relationship

James Garbarino, educator of brain science at Loyola University Chicago, calls attention to that parental rights are affected by individual and open perspectives of child-guardian connections. Are children:

- The private property of parents,
- Individuals from families with no immediate connection to the state, or
- Natives with an essential association with the state?

Children as Private Property

Parental rights have turn into the most secured and appreciated of every Constitutional right. They are in light of the characteristic right to bring forth children and the probability that love leads parents to act to the greatest advantage of their children. The Fourth Amendment's security of the protection of the home and the Fourteenth Amendment's expected procedure provision are translated to give parents lawful and physical guardianship of their children. The famous assumption that children are the property of their parents accordingly is reasonable.

In the 1995 Congress, a Parental Rights and Responsibilities Act was presented. It would have made a Constitutional alteration indicating outright parental rights. It didn't accumulate support in light of the fact that the lawful framework as of now regards parental rights. It additionally would have made shielding children from disregard and ill-use more troublesome.

Disregarding firmly held convictions despite what might be expected; the legitimate framework no more considers children as property. There even is a hereditary premise for the legitimate position that parents don't claim their children. The qualities we give them are not our own. Our own particular qualities were blended when they were transmitted to us by our parents. Our qualities are outside our ability to control. We truly don't possess them. They reach out back through past eras and conceivably forward into future eras. We are just the makeshift caretakers of our own qualities and of our children.

It holds that a singular's entitlement to replicate and a guardian's wishes can't be the essential establishment of family law. The essential center must be on children's necessities and hobbies. The guardian child relationship is one of stewardship. Parental power includes obligations past the guardian's own particular wishes.

In addition, our legitimate framework is taking into account the rule that no individual is qualified for own another person. Gatekeepers of bumbling grown-ups are operators, not proprietors, of those persons. In the same way, the childrearing privileges of parents comprise of 1) the guardianship right (legitimate care) to settle on choices for a child and 2) the privilege to physical authority of the child. These rights are in view of a child's advantage and needs as opposed to responsibility for child. We unquestionably don't claim our children.

Children as Family Members

Children are by and large viewed as relatives with no immediate connection to the state. The idea of parental rights sprang from customs and Constitutional points of reference that invest hereditary and new parents with unique rights.

Parental rights are legitimate privileges taking into account the ethical and social equality of children to be supported and secured. They are in light of the presumption that parents can best choose how to bring up a child without undue obstruction by the state. Without a willful or automatic relinquishment of parental obligations, the state can't for all time expel children from their parents' care to look for a superior home for them unless there has been a lawful end of parental rights.

Children as Citizens

Two patterns have included the perspective of a child as a subject. The main is the developing accentuation on the privilege of children to grow up without disregard or misuse. The second is expanded limits on parental control found in child disregard and misuse laws, child work laws, obligatory instruction laws, pre-adult social insurance arrangements and parental obligation laws. At the point when parents don't satisfy their obligations, child security administrations intercede and legislative organizations can accept lawful and physical care. At that point the child's essential relationship is with the state as overseer.

Like different gatekeepers, parents have the legitimate privilege to settle on stewardship choices. Society for the most part concedes to their power. The test is to urge parents to act in light of a legitimate concern for their children instead of in their own particular narrow minded hobbies. Toward this end, legislators depend on influence and instruction to help parents satisfy their commitments. Since they are inert to influence and instruction, a few parents' required lawful mediations previously, even after the fact an infant is conceived.

The Parent-Society Contract

It asserts that parental rights don't have an immediate Constitutional premise. The rise of children's rights mirrors this position; our general public has logically and exactly constrained the control parents have over their children's lives.

Dwyer embraces the Enlightenment see that persons who imagine and conceive an offspring enter a certain agreement with society to bring up their children as mindful natives. Harm brought about by abuse broadens past the people included and gives our general public a convincing enthusiasm for the wellbeing of our young.

Additionally holds that a guardian's commitments get from a certain agreement with the state past the child. This guardian culture contract gives an in number good basic to open endeavors that guarantee each child's wellbeing and personal satisfaction. Since an agreement infers common commitments, the parents and society are responsible to one another. The administration's part is reflected in level headed discussions about:

- Child wellbeing. Is it a privilege? Is it a benefit? An apparatus for social control? The pattern is to view it as a privilege.

- Adolescent childbirth. Who has lawful and physical guardianship of a minor's infant? Entirely talking nobody, yet relatives and government approaches bolster minor parents naturally.

- Financial backing. Is money related obligation regarding a child absolutely a private matter or an open obligation? Both. Government and state laws command childrearing advantages notwithstanding money related child support from parents and at times grandparents.

In the guardian culture contract, government assumes an imperative part in supporting parents in raising children and averting abuse. The closeness included in family connections can't be given by the state. It's the obligation of families to back children. Still, state and neighborhood governments are in charge of giving schools and safe neighborhoods to bolster childrearing. They can give wellbeing protection, charge conclusions and welfare advantages also.

Parents truly needn't bother with particularly characterized rights. They have rights that spill out of their children's rights. Lamentably, parental privileges and children's rights don't fit well in contemporary society. As illustrations, work environments offer little convenience for parents' childrearing obligations, and, when children are held uncertainly in apparently brief child care, their entitlement to able parents is unfulfilled.

Open strategies must perceive that children have the privilege to be watched over by persons with a persevering duty to, and the limit for, parenthood. Open strategies additionally need to perceive that in the guardian culture contract, society must guarantee that parents have entry to key childrearing assets. The parental rights level headed discussion would be determined by moving it from children as property to parenthood as a profession. Parenthood is a guardian culture, contract-based profession with rights got from the obligation to support a child and to backer for the child's advantage.

Being the adoring mother or father of a child does not so much imply that one is met all requirements for lawful and physical custodial rights. Parental adoration is inadequate for sound child improvement. A minor or formatively impaired individual can be an adoring mother or father without having parental rights. Persons even remain a mother or a father of a child after parental rights have been ended and different parents have expected motherhood and fatherhood parts through selection or family relationship care.

The Rights of Mothers

The laws of each state give the lady or young lady who imagines and bears a child programmed acknowledgment as the legitimate mother. Conceiving an offspring takes after the physical relationship shaped amid pregnancy. These laws mirror a properly solid inclination for conception mothers, particularly the individuals who nurture and structure connection bonds with their infants. This is convoluted by surrogates who are not hereditary mothers but rather who have a pre-birth physical association with an infant.

States from time to time challenge hereditary/conception motherhood unless convincing circumstances emerge, for example, a Child in Need of Protective Services appeal documented before childbirth. Indeed, even in such cases, an infant may be put in child care under state authority with the goal of restoring the hereditary/conception mother. This plan as a rule is not understood. A comparable circumstance exists with children whose mothers are imprisoned with the desire of keeping up the mothers' guardianship of their children. A recent report by Volunteers of America uncovered that after arrival of their mothers from jail 81% of their children stayed with their parental figures and did not live with their mothers.

Ladies and young ladies who conceive an offspring can decrease parenthood by willful disavowal of their parental rights through a Termination of Parental Rights continuing to take into consideration selection. Incomprehensibly, verifiable acknowledgment that minors don't have the judgment needed for parenthood is reflected in the way that minors oblige a gatekeeper notice item so as to end their parental rights and a grown-up or institutional payee to get Temporary Aid to Families with Dependent Children advantages. An automatic Termination of Parental Rights can be started after sensible endeavors to help parents meet return conditions have fizzled. Mothers' parental rights likewise can be ended consequently at childbirth under circumstances, for example, past automatic terminations or homicide of a kin. In a few states, outsiders like non-permanent parents can appeal to for the end of hereditary parental rights.

The Rights of Fathers

Not at all like maternity, has significant Constitutional direction been given to states in deciding paternity. States must protect that men have the chance to look to set up paternity. A hereditary association and an association with a child (or the push to build up one) are essential for Constitutional assurance of a paternity claim.

To claim parental rights, guys must enlist with putative father registries inside of changing time spans. Offices are obliged to inform putative fathers of the mothers' selection arranges. Inquiries emerge about the achievability of making fathers mindful of their need to enroll. In circumstances where hereditary fathers would prefer not to recognize fatherhood, state organizations attempt to set up paternity through hereditary testing, other natural proof or affirmation by the mother or the father so as to look for child bolster installments.

A father's hereditary tie can be overridden when a child's advantage are better served by a man who is hitched to the mother and who has set up an association with the child. In the 1989 U.S. Incomparable Court case Michael H. v. Gerald D., the hereditary father of a child created amid a two-faced relationship was precluded paternity in support from claiming the father who was really bringing up the child.

Parental Liability

The normal law principle of parental insusceptibility has looked after that, without persistent and wanton wrongdoing, children can't sue their parents for carelessness. In light of the greatness of child disregard and misuse, most states and courts are starting to characterize parental risk. As long prior as 1963, an Illinois Appeals Court heard Zepeda v. Zepeda in which a child sued his father for having made him resulting from wedlock. In spite of the fact that that suit was unsuccessful, it raised the issue of a child's legitimate right to be needed, cherished and supported... basically, to be ably parented.

Children have effectively sued their parents for carelessness and host brought activities against third gatherings that estrange a guardian from the crew. In 1992 in Orlando, Florida, eleven-year-old Gregory Kingsley lawfully "separated" his mother so he could be received by his non-permanent parents.

The Parens Patriae Doctrine

The most huge reality supporting state inclusion is that children don't pick the families into which they are conceived. The parens patriae tenet legitimizes state intercession as a piece of the guardian culture contract. Parens patriae is Latin for "father of the individuals." The tenet concedes the characteristic force and power of the state to ensure individuals who are legitimately not able to follow up for their own benefit. It gives state courts a definitive energy to end parental rights and is in view of three presumptions:

- Childhood and pre-adulthood are times of reliance and oblige supervision.

- The family is of essential significance however the state ought to assume a part in a child's training and mediate when the family neglects to give sufficient nurturance, good preparing or supervision.

- When parents differ or neglect to practice their power, the fitting power to focus a child's or a youthful advantage is an open authority. The parens patriae convention enables the state to urge parents and minors to act in ways that are useful to society. It never assumed that the state would accept child rearing capacities. Rather, the state is in charge of securing the best advantage of children under the direction of two standards:

- The wellbeing of society relies on children being instructed and not being abused.

- A child's formative requirements for nurturance and insurance are characterized by child disregard and misuse statutes.

A 1985 choice by Canada's Supreme Court made a child's welfare fundamental in question between hereditary parents and outsiders. In King v. Low, the Court expressed that despite the fact that the hereditary parents' cases would get genuine thought, they must offer route to the best advantage of the children when the children have grown close mental ties with another person. This perspective is grabbing hold in American courts also.

Our lawful framework recognizes what parents can do to themselves and what they can do to their children. For instance, parents can reject key therapeutic treatment themselves yet more often than not aren't permitted to do likewise with their children. They likewise aren't allowed to physically hurt their children, nor would they be able to permit children to physically hurt themselves.

Parents who neglect to give a base level of consideration, who surrender their children or who neglect to give supervision can be discovered blameworthy of disregard. Parents who physically, candidly or sexually misuse their children can be discovered blameworthy of ill-use. Parents who have been declared guilty a genuine wrongdoing, who misuse medications or liquor or who can't meet return conditions after their children have been evacuated can be discovered unfit as parents. At the point when persons can't be influenced or taught to wind up capable parents inside of a certain time of time, parental rights can be ended to empower reception.

State Liability

In spite of the parens patriae tenet, the risk of the state on the off chance that it doesn't ensure minors has not been obviously characterized. In l989, the U.S. Preeminent Court administered in DeShaney v. Winnebago County Department of Social Services that the state is not needed by the Fourteenth Amendment to ensure the life, freedom or property of its nationals against attack by private on-screen characters.

A redrafting court in California maintained a neighborhood court's release of a suit by a seventeen-year-old who claimed harm by blunder of his appropriation as an infant:

Dennis asserted that the Department carelessly or purposefully neglected to take sensible activities to achieve his selection. Subsequently, he was denied of legitimate and viable parental consideration and direction and a safe family environment. Dennis asserted that this brought on him mental and passionate harm.

The rejection of Dennis' objection was maintained in redrafting court on various grounds, incorporating the trouble in specifically connecting his harm to the inability to organize his selection. The court inferred that risk could come about with all the more persuading connections between right on time background and later results.

In December of 1981, lawyers for the State of Illinois and Cook County paid $150,000 in an out-of-court settlement of a suit of a previous ward child, Billy Nichols, who had been endowed to the child-welfare framework and later as a grown-up sued the region social administration office for the carelessness of social laborers that kept Billy reliant and unfit to live in the public eye.

On September l9, l960, Billy and his seven-month-old sister were deserted by their mother and discovered eating waste behind a the dumps column mission in Chicago. Billy's age (more or less five) was obscure, and his discourse was ambiguous. He was sent to an organization for the hindered in Michigan for a long time. After an ensuing stormy foster-home position, he was set in Cook County's adolescent security jail for almost three years, in spite of the fact that the administrator over and over requested of the court to uproot him.

In l969, a legitimate guide legal counselor, Pat Murphy, recorded a class-activity suit to discharge subordinate and disregarded children from jail for Billy. At 14, Billy was exchanged to Elgin State Hospital, where he fled ten times and was focused on the Illinois Security Hospital at Chester at 18 years old. After three years Attorney Murphy mediated to select Nichols in a psychiatric system for a long time, until he was imprisoned for auto robbery.

The Right to be a Competent Parent

To say that a guardian has a privilege to be capable may extend the thought of rights too far. Notwithstanding, the rationale for this right in our general public is convincing and worth considering.

Above all else, by definition the child-guardian unit is irreducible. One a large portion of the unit is a guardian, and one half is a child. The hobbies of children and the hobbies of parents are as one, and both get from a child's objective of dependable citizenship.

At the point when parents face hazardous situations, neediness, unemployment, disease or mental insufficiencies, their children inexorably confront the same issues alongside the danger of awkward child rearing. On the off chance that children's advantage are to be satisfied, the hobbies of parents must likewise be considered. In the event that children have an ethical right to be capably parented, then parents have an ethical right to be capable in the event that they are not under the legitimate or physical care of others.

A second reason is that the honesty of society itself relies on equipped parents. Uncouth parents undermine the strength of society and acquire huge open expenses. Consequently, in this perspective turning into an able guardian merits the status of a privilege.

Third, individuals have a hereditary inclination to parent skillfully so as to guarantee the survival of our species. The objective of the conceptive cycle is parenthood, not simply reproduction.

Considering and conceiving an offspring start parenthood as the realization of the parents' own formative phases of childhood, immaturity and adulthood. In the most central sense, skillful parenthood satisfies the part of a lady or a man in the regenerative cycle. So as to save humankind and our general public, grown-ups have a privilege to satisfy their conceptive and parental possibilities and for the state to help them get to be able parents when conceivable.

Adjusting the Rights of Parents and Minors

The embodiment of childhood toward the start of the Twentieth Century was its reliance. Skilled parents regarded this reliance by reasonably practicing their power. In the second 50% of the Twentieth Century, parental power declined.

Therefore, childrearing has turn into an arrangement in the middle of guardian and child with state and different offices checking the procedure.

Previously, children were accepted to have abilities we now infrequently think they have on the grounds that their work was expected to help a family survive. In our endeavors to give our children pleasant childhoods, we have a tendency to minimize their formative need to accept obligations and commitments. Much disarray about youthfulness is brought on by unpleasant clashes between teenagers' rights and their commitments to their parents. This highlights minors' obligation to acknowledge parental power and to chip in with their parents.

In a few ways, the contemporary pre-adult mission for freedom speaks to an arrival to the time in which childhood did not develop past fourteen. The distinction is that in prior hundreds of years persons were financially beneficial at fourteen years old and were not fit for multiplication though now they have an expanding number of years, regularly past adulthood, before they turn out to be monetarily profitable.

Parent power - the prime hope for a grass roots revival of English education

This is my third investigative report into the parlous condition of training in England's state schools. The initially contended for a monstrous decrease in the size of government intercession; the second for an exchange of energy to give educators much more control of the training procedure. Presently, in this last article, I need to highlight the basic part that can, and ought to, be played by parents, grandparents and nearby groups in helping adolescents add to their individual abilities and aptitudes, so they are not only prepared to win a living, but rather all the more altogether to appreciate a satisfying life and make a significant commitment to the general public they will inevitably acquire..

Much is said today of the need to engage children and give them more control of the way their schools are run. This is an important practice in majority rules system as children developed, however should never be presented in a manner which debilitates educator self-sufficiency and classroom discipline. One of the administration's late things of reserved alcove window dressing is 'Understudy Voice', a project which welcomes children to rate their instructors' execution. This, they now acknowledge, gives youths the chance to downsize educators whom they judge to be excessively strict. Under this new activity they're additionally offered the shot of talking planned new educators, one candidate being embarrassed by a solicitation to sing his main tune. Absurd approaches like these have prompted a checked decrease in control in schools. For all intents and purposes consistently there is a rough assault on an instructor in England. One fourteen-year-old kid sexually attacked a classroom aide. The head needed him removed, however the governors upset his choice. A twelve year old kid was banned from an Essex school for conveying a blade, yet was permitted back by an offers board. With this careless order, children will annoy with exemption, and believe that they can do likewise when they leave school which is scarcely what we need.

Children are being taught their rights, however not their obligations. Coordination Group Publications, one of the UK's biggest instructive distributers, has sold a huge number of duplicates of 'Your Legal Rights', a book which guarantees teens: 'You have the privilege to be shielded from passionate or physical ill-use'. One of the illustrations it gives of physical misuse is being made to join in a cross-country run. This was once thought to be a superb method for getting fit, however unmistakably our point now is not to urge young people to keep up an abnormal state of physical wellness, yet to have the capacity to take their place in a suit society. Children if we enabled, however in the meantime they must be urged to perceive power, and inevitably accept positions of power, for as Voltaire focused on, "firm train serves to rebuff the guilty party, as well as to 'urge the others' to stay idealistic."

Expecting that power can be tweaked from the administration, and a vast measure exchanged to educators and senior students, some must be held and reassigned to parents and neighborhood groups. Parents are lawfully in charge of their children, and since they pay the heft of the duties which finance the state instruction framework, they ought to have an intense voice in the way that cash is spent. In a majority rule government there ought to be no tariff without direct representation, as the Bostonians natives contended when they looked down on the British government and held their exceptionally fruitful Tea Party challenge. There's little uncertainty that if a submission were held today, parents would vote against the unbending, exam based 3Rs national syllabus, for a more liberal, assorted and adaptable educational module which took account of children's necessities, as well as of instructors' individual abilities and enthusiasms. Classes must be versatile, so they can react to a child's characteristic interest, whether it's a hobby is grasshoppers or an enthusiasm for gathering outside coins. So much educating today is dull, and bears little relationship to this present reality. An emphasis on breezing through tests does little to cultivate innovativeness, eagerness and an enthusiasm for lifetime study. At five the larger part of children can hardly wait to get the chance to class; at sixteen most can hardly wait to leave. Training ought to come back to its etymological roots. It ought to be a procedure of drawing out (from the Latin educare), as opposed to a careless administration of inculcation. Over the long haul the main important instruction is self-training, for what children learn at school today will be outdated in a couple of years time.

The instructive desires of legislators fizzle, not on the grounds that they're too high, but rather on the grounds that they're set so horrifyingly low. A solid training framework needs assorted qualities as opposed to brain desensitizing congruity. Families ought to be given the decision of sending their children to specialized schools, comprehensives, confidence schools, auxiliary current, language structure schools or government funded schools. Alternately, on the off chance that they have sufficient energy and capacity, why would it be advisable for them to be prevented from joining the evaluated twenty to fifty thousand parents in England who choose to show their posterity at home? Once more, is there any good reason why parents shouldn't in England be given the opportunity to open 'free schools'? This has been finished with incredible achievement in Sweden where since 1955 nearby groups have the flexibility to purchase a fitting building and transform it into a free school. Parents are given a voucher to pay for their child's instruction and can trade it in for money at any school they favor, inasmuch as it doesn't charge any sort of 'top up' expenses. Since this enactment was presented well more than a thousand free schools have opened and now teach more than one in ten of all Swedish understudies.

Accomplishment in life is not firmly identified with IQ scores, but rather is all the more personally connected with identity variables, similar to determination, amiability, creativity, valor and inspiration. Examination demonstrates that talented children have a tendency to be masterful, musical, great at games, ready to correspond effortlessly with grown-ups, have an energetic and unique creative ability combined with a capacity to concentrate all alone hobbies instead of just what is being taught in the school educational module. Parents have been persuaded that instruction is about picking up recognitions and degrees, which are the reason a large portion of the children at London state schools, are presently accepting private educational cost to help them through their SATs and GCSEs. Children's psyches ought not to be packed with certainties. They ought to be offered time to dream, which is the open sesame to innovativeness. Like the White Queen in Alice in Wonderland they ought to be urged to feel that instruction incorporates accepting about six inconceivable things each morning before breakfast. At a decent school, children ought to be prepared to cooperate for the benefit of everyone instead of in ascetic detachment. This is not happening today in most UK schools as per a late study of eight nations where an example of children was requested that answer to the announcement: 'The majority of the understudies in my class are benevolent and supportive.' In Switzerland more than eighty for each penny of children answered that this was valid; in Britain just 43 for every penny of children gave the same certifiable reaction, the least of the considerable number of nations surveyed. This is a dismal analysis on our schools, and a considerably sadder impression of the condition of our separated society.

Numerous autonomous schools have a social administration program, an additional curricular movement which urges senior young men to go out into the group: to visit the elderly in their homes, do their shopping, help at day focuses, work in philanthropy shops, take sustenance and garments to vagrants and work at places for the rationally impeded. By doing as such they pick up as much as the individuals they serve. Why can't a comparative framework be presented in state schools? Cultivating is another important additional curricular movement, which can be completed under the supervision of parents and grandparents at whatever point there's an open plot of apportioning area. Under two years back the Royal Horticultural Society dispatched a Campaign for Schools Gardening, which well more than six thousand schools have now joined. Its target is to give each young person the chance to get a preference for planting, and the chance to develop and find out about plants. Children ought to likewise be required to perform errands, an obligation which sets them up for the obligations of grown-up life. This is the conviction of the philanthropy help line www.parentlineplus.org.uk which guarantees that and being a certainty developer, 'Errands can likewise show children how to arrange their own particular time, mulling over others' needs'. This used to be underestimated in many families, however is presently to a great extent overlooked, unless children are paid off to run an errand or clean the family auto. A study did by Markella Rutherford, a right hand teacher of humanism at Wellesley College, Massachusetts, uncovered that American child rearing magazines consistently prompted families to give children routine assignments, such as improving, shopping, house cleaning, planting and nursing wiped out relatives. This counsel vanished from the magazines in the 1980s. From that point forward, children's just obligation is to get their work done. This is deplorable, since the more trust we put in children, the more they will develop to legitimize that trust. Learning doesn't stop when we finish our formal instruction, for as Maimonides, the colossal medieval Jewish savant certified: 'A man ought to never quit adapting, even on his last day.' To perceive and advance the uniqueness of the student, and set them up for a lifetime of investigation and development, we must perceive and advance the distinction of every individual school.

The importance of early childhood education

The best indicator of a decent consummation is a decent starting. The old aphorism is a genuine today as when it was initially articulated such a long time ago that nobody can unmistakably say who first talked those words. Regarding the training of youthful children this maxim has such colossal significance that it is difficult to exaggerate its significance. All learning and background is shaped by what happens to the child in the early years of his or her life. The impact of the family is of significant significance however the impact of the instructive open doors offered to youthful children is pretty much as intense and, in a few ways, all the more effective. For it is the effect of ahead of schedule childhood instruction that decides the disposition a child will take to formal educating at essential or optional level.

The world today is a grieved spot. We appear to be showing signs of improvement at loathing each other. We appear to be less and less ready to acknowledge individuals who are unique in relation to us. In a world loaded with roughness, wrongdoing, harassing, disarray and capriciousness we need to ask some imperative inquiries. Can any anyone explain why a few children

- Try not to wind up vicious?
- Try not to wind up spooks?
- Try not to wind up discouraged?
- Don't opposed themselves as well as other people?

- Try not to gloom and abandon life?

These may not be the most significant inquiries being postured in today's reality however they are among the most imperative. Where would we be able to swing to perceive the responses to these inquiries? What do we realize that can help us unload the issues installed in them and go to a dream of how to bring up and instruct youthful children?

The responses to these and different inquiries regarding children are rising up out of new research about how the human cerebrum develops and creates. Despite the fact that we are far off knowing precisely who we can counteract roughness and despondency we have taken in a decent arrangement about how to cultivate the mind's potential as an organ to help children develop to end up contributing and gainful individuals from society. Before we investigate a portion of the suggestions from this examination we have to quickly survey the five ranges of advancement that all children go through amid childhood.

Understanding Child Development

There are five territories of advancement that children experience as they develop to be youthful grown-ups. These strides show up in a somewhat unsurprising succession, consistently. They are not care for ventures of a step prompting increasingly elevated levels. Maybe, they are similar to a winding of stages through which a child cycles interminably as they develop and developed. Eventually the most elevated amount of fulfillment may not be come to in a given territory but rather that does not mean the child can't advance to different ranges of the winding.

The five regions of child advancement are:

- Physical
- Intellectual
- Linguistic
- Emotional
- Social

They can be effortlessly recalled by the utilization of the somewhat heartbreaking acronym "Heaps".

a) Physical Development

This range of child improvement is undoubtedly the simplest to comprehend and watch. Physical improvement incorporates: gross engine aptitudes, fine engine abilities, engine control, engine coordination and kinaesthetic criticism. We should clarify each of these quickly.

Gross engine abilities are those developments of the extensive muscles of the legs, trunk and arms.

Fine engine abilities are the developments of the little muscles of the fingers and hands.

Motor control is the capacity to move these extensive and little muscles.

Motor coordination is the capacity to move these muscles in a smooth and liquid example of movement.

Kinaesthetic input is the body's capacity to get data to the muscles from the outer environment so the individual knows where his body is situated in space.

b) Scholarly Development

This region identifies with the level of insight of a child by and large and to the different parts of knowledge that impact general level of general capacity. Among these numerous angles are:

Verbal abilities are our capacity to correspond with words our thoughts, state of mind, convictions, musings and feelings.

Non-verbal abilities are our capacity to utilize visual and spatial-perceptual aptitudes to decipher our general surroundings.

Attention-compasses the capacity to manage an emphasis on a jolt for an adequate time of time to decipher it and comprehend it.

Concentration-our capacity to use consideration regarding juggle boosts into different changes as important to break down it precisely.

Visual-engine abilities the capacity to arrange the developments of the eyes and hands to control questions adequately.

Visual-perceptual aptitudes the capacity to break down jolts outwardly without essentially controlling them physically.

Memory-can be sound-related or visual (or even kinaesthetic as on account of recollect move steps) and can be separated into some vital sub-sorts:

- Immediate review capacity to hold info sufficiently long to review it straight away if needed to do as such

- Short-term memory-capacity to hold include more than a more drawn out time of time, maybe minutes or hours

- Long-term memory-capacity to store information and review is well after it has been seen, maybe days or months, even years after the fact

c) Semantic Development

Semantic advancement alludes to dialect use. Like different regions of child advancement it can be separated into sub-sorts.

Receptive dialect our capacity to comprehend talked dialect when we hear it

Expressive dialect our capacity to utilize talked dialect to convey to others

Pragmatic dialect the capacity to comprehend amusingness, incongruity, mockery and know how to react proper to what another has said or asked and additionally know when to hold up and tune in

Self-talk-the capacity to utilize inside, quiet dialect to thoroughly consider issues, adapt to challenges and delay motivations

Reasoning-the capacity to thoroughly consider issues, for the most part with self-talk yet at different times so anyone might hear, make arrangements of activity utilizing words

Creative intuition albeit not entirely an etymological capacity I incorporate it here in light of the fact that numerous individuals use dialect inventively, in new and innovative ways.

d) Enthusiastic Development

This part of improvement, alongside social advancement, is most likely a standout amongst the most underrated yet most imperative parts of figuring out how to live on the planet. Regardless of how superb scholarly, physical and phonetic advancement may be we are destined to lead lives of dissatisfaction and troublesome in the event that we have not increased agreeable enthusiastic improvement. It incorporates:

Frustration resilience the capacity to adapt adequately when things don't go the way we need or anticipate

Impulse control-the capacity to think before we act and not do everything that comes into our head

Anger administration capacity to determine clash without response to verbal or physical brutality

Inter-individual knowledge understanding the mentality, convictions and inspirations of others

Intra-individual insight comprehend our own particular disposition, convictions and inspirations

e) Social Development

Sharing-knowing how to request that utilization the materials that fit in with another

Turn-taking-knowing when the ball is in your court to do something and when to inquire as to whether you can do it

Cooperation-the abilities of working with others towards a gathering objective of undertaking

Collaboration-the capacity to correspondence your data in an important manner when working with others.

Again it is important to rehash that enthusiastic and social improvement assume a gigantically essential part in our capacity to lead lives of poise and admiration. They likewise generally decide how well we will coexist with workmates, supervisors and friends and family including life-accomplices.

When we perceive that all children go through every range of improvement we plan instructive project for them that are formatively suitable. Most preschools have done recently that.

Shockingly numerous early years settings succumb to weight and push children towards scholastic objectives and destinations, infrequently fanatically. For sure, the educational program in our lesser and senior newborn child classes is to a great extent formatively improper. It is unreasonably educator and guardian focused and extremely little child-focused. Notwithstanding, proper or wrong, it is insufficient to concentrate on child advancement alone in our work with youthful children. We must start to perceive the characteristic potential bolted inside of the child's cerebrum.

The Human Brain

Bolted inside the mind are the possibilities that make us human. We are conceived with the potential for:

- Love Hate
- Patience Mistrust
- Tenderness Violence
- Hope Despair
- Trust Suspicion
- Dignity Corruption
- Respect Revenge

It is the obligations of grown-ups to open the positive possibilities of the mind and keep the negative from showing up.

Every instructive experience of children in the early years, in fact every single instructive experience of children over the whole school years, must place an accentuation on discharging the positive potential that exists in the mind. Late mind research, quite a bit of it directed by Dr. Bruce Perry in Texas, has lit up six center qualities, each of them identified with mind development and improvement that must be a concentrate being developed proper instructive projects for youthful children.

The Six Core Strengths

Bruce Perry and his partners at the Child Trauma Academy in Texas have distinguished six qualities that are identified with the anticipated arrangement of cerebrum development and improvement. These six qualities, if sustained and encouraged properly, will help a child develop to turn into a gainful individual from society. They are:

- Attachment

- Self-regulation

- Affiliation

- Attunement

- Tolerance

- Respect

- Connection

The principal of the six center qualities happens in earliest stages. It is the adoring bond between the newborn child and the essential guardian. Early connection scholars' conceiver of the essential parental figure as the mother yet it is presently perceived that it could too be the father, grandparent or any adoring individual. The essential supplier, when giving steady and unsurprising supporting to the baby makes what is known as a "protected" connection. This is proficient in that cadenced move in the middle of baby and guardian; the adoring nestles, embraces, grins and commotions that go in the middle of parental figure and newborn child. Should this move be out of step, capricious, profoundly conflicting or confused a "frail" connection is shaped. At the point when connections are secure the baby discovers that it is adorable and cherished, that grown-ups will give sustain and consideration and that the world is a protected spot. At the point when connection is shaky the baby takes in the inverse.

As the child develops from a base of secure connection he or she gets to be prepared to love and be a companion. A protected connection makes the ability to shape and keep up solid enthusiastic bonds with another. Connection is the format through which we see the world and individuals in it.

Self-Regulation

Self-regulation is the ability to think before you act. Little children are bad at this, they realize this ability as they develop on the off chance that they are guided via minding grown-ups who demonstrate to them best practices to stop and think. Self-regulation is the capacity to observe our essential inclinations, for example, hunger, end, solace and control them. As it were, it is the capacity to put off delight and sit tight for it to arrive. Great self-regulation anticipates outrage upheavals and fits and helps us adapt to dissatisfaction and endure stress. It is an existence ability that must be found out and, similar to all the center qualities, its establishes are in the neuronal associations profound inside the mind.

Association

Association is the paste of solid human connections. At the point when children are instructed in a domain and encourages positive companion collaborations through play and innovative gathering learning ventures they build up the quality of alliance. It is the capacity to "join in" and work with others to make something more grounded and more enduring than is generally made by one individual alone. Alliance makes it conceivable to deliver something more grounded and more inventive than is expert by one alone. Association brings into the child's mindfulness that he or she is not an only I but rather a "We" together.

Attunement

Attunement is the quality of seeing past ourselves. It is the capacity to perceive the qualities, needs, values and hobbies of others. Attunement starts rather basically in childhood. A child first perceives that I am a young lady, he is a kid. Through the early years of training it turns out to be more nuanced: he is from India and preferences distinctive nourishment than I, she is from Kenya and talk with an alternate accent than I. Attunement helps children see similarities instead of contrasts in light of the fact that as the child advances from seeing diverse shading skin and distinctive methods for talking he or she starts to perceive that individuals are more comparative than diverse. That conveys us to the following center quality.

Resilience

At the point when the child adds to the center quality of attunement it discovers that distinction isn't generally all that imperative. The child discovers that distinction is effectively endured. Through this taking in the child builds up the mindfulness that is contrast that unites every single individual. Resilience relies on upon attunement and obliges tolerance and a chance to live and learn with individuals who at first look appear to be "changed". We must beat the trepidation of contrast to end up tolerant.

Regard

The last center quality is admiration. Appreciation is a long lasting formative procedure. Admiration stretches out from appreciation of self to regard of others. It is the last center quality to create, obliges a fitting domain and a chance to meet a mixture of individuals. Honest to goodness admiration praises differing qualities and searches it out. Children who regard other children, who have built up this center quality, don't modest far from individuals who appear to be changed. A domain in which numerous children are gathered together to learn, investigate and play will encourage the center quality of appreciation.

How the Brain Grows

The cerebrum develops from the base to the top. Each of the center qualities is identified with a stage and site of mind development. In early stages connection bonds are obtained and set down enthusiastic flags profound inside of the cerebrum. In the meantime the mind stem is seeing to it that substantial capacities can act naturally managed. Later on in childhood the enthusiastic focuses of the cerebrum go under expanding control so hissy fits vanish and the child controls their passionate life. In mid-childhood the child's mind starts to add to the ability to think and consider the outside environment. It is at this stage when the frontal zones of the mind start to develop and it is at this stage in cerebrum development when the center qualities of association, attunement, resilience and admiration can develop also.

The Classroom and the Brain's Core Strengths

The instruction of youthful children must be attempted on account of the center qualities.

Classrooms where there is peace and congruity among a wide assortment of children will make open doors for connection, resilience and admiration to create. These classroom must be portrayed by play, innovative investigation of items, lessons which are movement based not instructor addressed. There must be test to the cerebrum as inventive lessons and instructing procedures. Agreeable learning exercises must be a piece of the school day. The classroom ought to periodically comprise of a chance to take part in helpful, blended capacity group work. There must be an open door for long haul, topical ventures to be investigated. The instructor ought to be an aide, continually educating because of the center qualities, continually watching children and seeing which of them need more structure and direction as they become through the center qualities. The educator should likewise be a man the children see as unsurprising and minding, patient and kind; a man who won't fanatically concentrate on errors.

Whose Responsibility is It?

We have discovered that the child's mind develops in an anticipated grouping and connected with this development are six center qualities for sound living on the planet. Each child is conceived with a mind having the possibility to full build up these center qualities. However every cerebrum must have a chance to interface with a classroom and home environment that encourages the improvement of these qualities. It is the obligation of grown-ups, especially parents and educators to hit the nail on the head.

BIRTH OF MY CHILDREN: THE JOY OF HUGGING MORE AND SCOLDING LESS

Thus, they develop and they change and they let go and they start to discover themselves. As your child forms into youthfulness she encounters what is ostensibly the most troublesome section of time in her life so far. Through this period she will encounter fast changes inside of her physicality, her mindfulness, her comprehension of her general surroundings, her connections, her own particular character, her vision without bounds, her own feeling of quality and reason,

85

her social life, her awareness of other's expectations... what's more, the rundown continues forever and on. This is both a traumatic and freeing time of move for her and you need to help her through it.

"Parents are some of the time a somewhat of a mistake to their children. They don't satisfy the guarantee of their initial years." Anthony Powell

This exceptionally sharp perception by Anthony Powell says all the more in regards to how your child will see you through her juvenile years than it does of you as a guardian. Try not to be excessively concerned; rather, discover some solace in realizing that she will be disillusioned in you regardless of how well you carry out your employment. Notwithstanding, on the off chance that you carry out your occupation well, she will rise up out of this drawn out time of edification with a solid measure of admiration and adoration for you that will help her to defeat her mistake of you.

So what goes ahead in the psyche of a juvenile?

It's a somewhat of a senseless question in a few regards, in light of the fact that we're all diverse. Be that as it may, child rearing your child through immaturity will oblige you to roll out improvements in your way to deal with her. The tenets of the diversion will change day by day and you will need to alter in the event that you are to stay in it.

It's regular for to parents make suppositions about their juvenile children. There is a propensity to review their own particular time of youth and accept that the considerations, sentiments and encounters they had in those days will give them an understanding into the psyches they could call their own children. To a certain degree that may work for you, yet it is so imperative to keep up an open line of correspondence with your child. On the off chance that she realizes that she won't be judged, overlooked or rejected when she opens up to you, she will be much more slanted to correspond with you. Maintain a strategic distance from sayings or overdone reactions to your child's correspondences with you - they are not really prone to serve both of you well.

In the event that she's stinging, and she tries to express that to you, the last words she needs to hear are 'you'll be fine'. Regardless of the possibility that said truly, they demonstrate little thought or heart-felt expression. She may not require extraordinary pearls of intelligence from you. She might just need you to listen - to ask her the amount she's stinging is or who it is that is hurt her. She might simply need to hang out and watch a film. Whatever she needs, it isn't an off-the-rack reaction. She needs to realize that you care and that you comprehend her. She needn't bother with "answers" constantly. Infrequently all that she needs is to be listened; to be 'got'; to realize that she's cherished.

Yet, understanding her doesn't give you an "Entrance All Areas" go to your child's internal identity. She is getting to be free of you now, so her insider facts are, by right, her privileged insights. On the off chance that she needs to impart them to you, she will, yet you don't have a privilege to make requests of exposure from her in light of the fact that she has as much right to her security as you do to yours. On the off chance that you don't permit her this flexibility she may withdraw and your line of correspondence will be lost - or possibly bargained.

Your youthful child is not altogether different from the little individual who you wearing a uniform for her first day of center school. What is distinctive is her recently discovered craving to be autonomous of you. These years may be as traumatic for you as they will be for her. You are needing to relinquish the individual you have invested years putting resources into and joining with.

You may surmise that she is getting to be thankless. It's more probable that she is diverted, overpowered and confounded. Be generous with her - she's going to need more beauty than you might suspect you have, yet in the event that you would prefer not to fizzle in this last phase of child rearing your child, you must discover it. Burrow profound - truly profound. She may well take more vitality out of you throughout the following 5-7 years as she has accomplished for the past 12-13 years.

Your child is adding to her own informal community now; one that has nothing to do with you. Indeed, even at 11 years old or 12 she may need to begin barring you so she can add to an existence far from you. These are the beginnings of her freedom. It's difficult for you however it is great. You need to give her a chance to do this and in the event that you can, attempt to encourage it. I permitted my children to have their companions around. They had their own rooms and those were their domain. This gave my children a feeling of autonomy and gave them a situation in which they could start to build up their own social lives.

Teenagers are brilliant. They have so much vitality, conviction, drive, desire and vision. Every one of these things need diverting in the event that they are to achieve their maximum capacity.

Your child hasn't all of a sudden turn out to be uncontrollable. Not on the off chance that you've brought her up well. She is more inclined to be attempting to discover the harmony between her reliance and autonomy. The individual she is and the individual she needs to be. This is a baffling time for her. She needs to be free of you however despite everything she needs you. She has no home she could call her own, she has no monetary freedom, and she has no vehicle. She needs you for these things and it disturbs her that she does. In what manner would she be able to be autonomous but destitute? It doesn't sit well with her. She will take her disappointments out on you on the grounds that she knows you will love her regardless. For some time, you will be her dash load up with the appalling countenances of misconception, dejection, disconnection, defenselessness and personality emergency stuck to it. Each time she tosses a dart, get it. Try not to give it a chance to infiltrate you and reason you torment. She is tossing without knowing why. It's not you she's going for - its the countenances on the dartboard.

Tolerance and resilience are extraordinary credits to be approaching at this time. Amid this time of turmoil for her, your serenity will be an appreciated remedy. It will help her to recapture her passionate harmony. On the off chance that you strike back or react violently to her apparently awful conduct you might just exacerbate the situation. Try not to toss the darts back at her (recollect that, they weren't went for you), lay them down. Be ease back to react. Be sensible. Tell her that you need to help her and that you are not out to win a battle. A delicate answer will help to extinguish the flame inside of her - inevitably. You won't generally get the response you covet however her heart will take it in and it will benefit her.

Each time you approach your child, do it from a position of enquiry as opposed to knowing and her reactions will better prepare you to comprehend her. Furnish her with the significant, asserting words and demonstrations of adoration that she longs for. Things that will pacify her disappointments recuperate her injuries, fill her vacancy, quiet the commotions, understand her disarrays and control her reasons for alarm.

Understanding your own psyche

As your child begins to tear herself far from you, the agony will get to be agonizing. You may feel rejected, ignored, disliked, affronted, undesirable, worthless.... You may start to feel that every one of these years of cherishing her, tending to her and putting resources into her have been a waste; that it was all worthless on the grounds that here she is, growing up and abandoning you without even such a great amount as a 'thank you', and what's more terrible, you don't have somebody to share your emotions with. Nobody with whom to talk through the troublesome time you are experiencing. Nobody who sees precisely what it is to be losing this child - your child. You are separated from everyone else.

She has discovered other individuals to share her existence with. She can't go to the film with you this Saturday - she's as of now orchestrated to run with another person. She needn't bother with you to plan supper for her today - she's now eaten. She won't be home tonight - she's staying with a companion. All of a sudden, she doesn't need you any longer.

You have been supplanted.

Supplanted by 'companions'. Individuals who did not comfort her when she was tragic; didn't take care of her when she was sick; didn't go up against her vacation consistently; didn't sustain her or dress her; didn't empty a lifetime of adoration into her. Who are these individuals? These fakers? What right do they need to detract your child from you? Why do they get the opportunity to "have" her unexpectedly? They've done nothing to merit her affection and commitment. You may be feeling furious, hurt, dispossessed, victimized, abandoned, and deserted .

Your intuition is to advise her how she is making you feel. You need her to realize that she owes you and that you don't should be dealt with thusly. You have earned her affection and appreciation. You need something back consequently for all the years you've given her. Truly? You think she owes you?

Did she request that be brought into this world? No. Did she not should be encouraged or dressed or adored? Yes. At the point when your child was conceived, you got to be obliged to her. She's presently breaking free. Liberated to be whoever she cravings to be. Allowed to carry on with the life she needs to live and there's nothing you can do aside from watch and trust. Your part as a guardian was to set her up for grown-up life. Since she is going after it, don't hold her back.

Take delight in realizing that her freedom from you is an indication of how well you have done your employment; that your speculation is paying off; that you have had huge impact in making her the individual that she is. Obviously you need to be cherished back - it will come, however don't request it. She needs to concentrate on herself for some time. Her self-centeredness is not wrong, yet it is unavoidable. She is attempting to discover her place on the planet. She must do this without anyone else - without you.

By the by, regardless she needs your direction and backing. You will feel objectified. That is the way youths can make you feel. Try not to stress, they don't remain as such. Continue cherishing her. Regardless she needs your affection despite the fact that you don't feel increased in value. Stay included as much as she needs you to yet don't meddle. Hold up in the wings until she approaches you. Keep on supporting her despite the fact that you feel your heart is breaking into pieces. Stay concentrated on her. This is a torrid time for you, however she is additionally battling and she can't be concerned with how you feel; she's not in charge of your emotions. Yes, you have to manage your own nervousness and agony, so require some investment out for yourself. Go to your companions or family, see a guide, join a care group, however for your child's purpose, don't offload your inconveniences onto her.

She is detecting an inlet opening up between you. How might you be able to conceivably know what she feels or considers? You're excessively old and withdrawn. She has her companions for that now. What used to be a family home is quick turning into a cabin, soup-kitchen and virtual ATM. She travels every which way however she sees fit; the TV remote far from you; has your supper with no much appreciated; secures herself away her space for a considerable length of time; takes each penny you have - to say the very least; abandons her clothing lying deliberately around her space for you to gather and lays the accuse immovably at your entryway if something isn't clean on a certain day; requests that you taxi her to her arrangements and lift her up again immediately - all of which you do affectionately, if not in some cases with a bit hurt. You need to be far beyond simply her taxi.

By what method would you be able to stay significant to her? By what method would you be able to still be a significant piece of her life? In what manner would you be able to stay associated with her? All things considered, a great approach to join this gathering is not to gatecrash but rather to get yourself welcomed, and on the off chance that you do get welcomed, to know your place. She needs to realize that you are still for her and that you haven't turn into her foe. Help her to remember this. Be a decent audience. Take an enthusiasm for all parts of her life. Offer to give her a lift to the silver screen as opposed to holding up to be inquired. Possibly clear your home occasionally with the goal that she can welcome her companions over (leave a lot of pizzas in the ice chest). Serve her, be liberal to her, luxurious her with affection. She won't demonstrate to you anyplace close to the sort of gratefulness you merit - possibly none at all occasionally, yet she won't close you out of her life either, on the grounds that she knows you mind.

The more she knows you mind, the more open she will be with you. Be that as it may, you have to stay extremely understanding and liberal for some time. You may find that a portion of the accompanying youthful intuition evokes genuine emotion with you:

1) You are to be the object of derision. This implies that you are to make yourself accessible to be chuckled at when her

companions are around. She must be permitted to ridicule you. Your taste in garments, music and hair-style are all up for gets. Go up against it the button and grin. It's your employment as the parental object of mocking. Be that as it may, she is not permitted to irreverence you. All must be done for entertainment only.

2) You may give sustenance at sure times. Young people are inclined to neglect to perform even the most key errands - including eating. Coercively feeding is not feasible however star dynamic procurement is permitted. Now and again, you may need to simply abandon it outside the room entryway.

3) You are to give cash to garments however may not go to the obtaining custom. This is saved for nearest companions just. Notwithstanding, when no companions are accessible, you may get an improvised welcome. Yet, be arranged to stay at home ought to a spur of the moment telephone call imply that your place has been given to the previously stated companion who is -'goodness delight!'- Abruptly free once more.

4) You are to embrace an adaptable demeanor with respect to concurrences with your youthful. The altering of her opinion in regards to all things is not out of the ordinary at all times. You may help her to remember her steady inability to

respect her understandings however don't expect much change for a couple of years - seeds lie in the ground quite a while before developing and proving to be fruitful.

5) You are to listen to all protests made against instructors at school while realizing that 99 times out of a hundred your child hasn't been hard done by and is probably at flaw for being restrained in school. In any case, keep a receptive outlook. There was more than one event when I needed to reprimand an educator for awful conduct towards my children. Make sure to urge your child to live inside of school laws, whether she concurs with them or not. This is a lesson forever. She

will need to figure out how to maintain laws and principles on the off chance that she is to fit into society - better that she discovers that now.

6) You will be the facilitator of no less than one hour of uproarious music being played consistently. For reasons unknown, youths wish to impart their music to you despite the fact that it may not be to your taste. After said hour, you may uphold a 23 hour boycott on uproarious music.

7) You might make your cell telephone accessible to her for crisis messaging when she has come up short on layaway on her telephone. Normal message sent:

"come up short on layaway, would you be able to get back to me?"

8) You will dry her removes when she has fallen with her companions everlastingly and a day (as a rule the "eternity" part gets overlooked). Really the 'and a day' frequently transforms into not as much as hour when she gets a telephone call while letting you know that she doesn't realize what she'd manage without you, and in a split second discovers her shreds have dried and she would much preferably make up with her companions than keep discovering solace in your arms. You're occupation - but a brief one - is finished.

9) You will stress, worry and frenzy when she goes AWOL. She will vanish for a

considerable length of time without letting you know where she is. She will go straight to a companion's home from school and overlook - yes, neglect to get back home. She will neglect to turn up for supper when you have affectionately set her up most loved feast, and call you to let you know she is eating out with companions when the table is now laid. You will frequently be discovered calling companions, family and the nearby healing facility to find her hours after she was expected home, while envisioning the most dire outcome imaginable, yet trusting and accepting through a tight midsection and tied stomach that she is alright. As she strolls through the entryway in the dead of night, totally uninformed of the pain she has created you through her negligence, and as you welcome her through tear-filled eyes and a heart loaded with help and outrage you will remain there shaking from head to toe making a decent attempt to chasten her, at long last succumbing to your urgent longing to hold her and never release her.

Not just did I permit my children to welcome companions back late during the evening, I would cook for them. I didn't attempt to include myself in the discussion; I stayed in the kitchen and tended to my own personal concerns unless I was welcome to join in, yet all the time I attempted to stay significant to my children by permitting them to act naturally while making myself accessible to be whatever I could be to them.

I didn't attempt to be their companion - I was their companion, however from a protected separation. Presently the ball was in my court to watch the limits and not venture over them. In the event that I did cross the limits I was made to know it in no unverifiable terms. In the event that they expected to talk, they could and I would tune in, however had I been a resolute, hard-lined, closed minded guardian, they most likely would not have felt the opportunity to impart their musings and emotions to me. I made the environment that permitted them to be expressive as opposed to attempting to compel them into corresponding and joining with me on my terms.

This magnanimity may make me sound like a push-over. Trust me, that is the exact opposite thing my children would call me. As per them, regardless of my 'cool'-ness, at the time I was still excessively unforgiving on them. I was demanding, outlandish, pitiless, harsh, and tyrannical and a large group of other appalling things.

I would demonstrate to them an awesome measure of resistance, comprehension and persistence however they never saw that. What they did see was my disappointment, disillusionment, outrage and agony at their rehashed nonchalance for my solicitations and limits and their own particular broken guarantees. I would tell them how baffled I was, and now and then tempers would flare on both sides. My inability to stay smooth all through some of our experiences didn't help me out - nor them, yet I generally apologized for any awful conduct on my part. In any case, I made certain they knew when I thought their conduct was impolite and unsatisfactory. They abhorred being informed that, yet where it counts they knew it was genuine and the seed was planted. Later, it would develop and prove to be fruitful - they in the end recognized that they comprehended what I had attempted to show them, yet they didn't concur with me on everything. Perhaps I wasn't right about everything.

Try not to attempt to be an "impeccable" guardian. You will fizzle. A savvy man once said 'no man is equivalent to his own talk'. In the event that you think for one minute that your child won't be frustrated in you then your desires of yourself may be too high. She more likely than not will be disillusioned in you, and she will tell you where you have fizzled, how you have missed the mark in your part as a guardian and how much better you could have been. Some of what she says will be valid. Whatever remains of it will basically originate from her own particular optimistic desires of the sort of individual she needed you to be and which you have neglected to be.

As injured and lacking as you may feel, you ought not take her feedback and frustration to heart. You may have tried your hardest, however even with the best resolve on the planet, it was never going to be sufficient; it was never going to be consummate. In any case, one thing you will have done as a decent parent is to furnish her to manage life's flaws - you being one of them.

In the long run, she will relinquish the failure and as your association with her proceeds into adulthood she will acknowledge in her development that the world is comprised of flawed individuals who go about existence in a defective way. In any case, she will bit by bit and consistently find the numerous fortunes that you have saved profound inside of her for the duration of her life and she will possible come to understand that even an imperfect precious stone has extraordinary quality.

When it at last sunrises, my children, having come to adulthood and every in their own particular time have let me know how they now see so a large portion of the things I had taught them however which they had not acknowledged at the season of being taught; that they had at last "seen" it. I can't help thinking that they have get through that difficult time of their lives furnished with great qualities, solid standpoints, charitable hearts and not a little shrewdness.

Obviously, much the same as me, they have their inadequacies, and, similar to me, they are on a journey. They will spend a lifetime attempting to better their own particular hearts and brains, managing one blemish at once. Much the same as I am doing. Our employment as parents isn't to "make" impeccable grown-ups. It is to guide our children into a method for living that we ourselves esteem yet which likewise permits them the opportunity to pick their own particular way and add to their own character. In the event that we have done that then we can solicit no more from ourselves and no a greater amount of them. We can be content with the information that notwithstanding our errors, weaknesses and blemishes, we have, all in all, not disappoint them and given them a decent start in life.

You won't generally be watchman to your child, yet you will dependably be her parent and you can likewise remain her companion. She won't require you in her life in the same way any longer, yet she may like to incorporate you. Should you neglect to arrange her youthful years with some affectability, a little quietude, a considerable measure of persistence, an immense measure of liberality and a lot of comprehension, you may miss the mark regarding giving her the complete childhood you had expected for her and which she merited. Try harder amid this sensitive and demanding time of her life. Nothing less will do.

In all that you do, comprehend this: that your part as a guardian is to instruct your child to end up autonomous of you - to help her to be free. Thus, onto the last piece of this section.

Giving up so your child can become By far a standout amongst the most fulfilling yet difficult encounters for a guardian is seeing her child develop into a grown-up. This is ostensibly, the most troublesome part of being a guardian -

having the craving to clutch what you adore most while realizing that to really cherish her, you must let her go. It is euphoric yet pitiful; invigorating yet terrifying; freeing yet segregating; satisfying yet discharging.

Your child - impending autonomous, is figuring out how to "be" without you. You must choose between limited options - let her. Try not to stick to her or she may push you away. Try not to dump your torment on her or she may dislike you for it. Yes, these progressions are excruciating for you as well however they are not your child's obligation.

The association with your child, which has been a more-than-noteworthy explanation behind your feeling of reason and satisfaction since she was conceived, is apparently attracting to the end. It has an inclination that it's all over bar, the yelling. She's growing up and getting prepared to fly and she's bringing your heart with her. You are encountering a sort of deprivation. The melancholy is overpowering. You are losing her.

Yet, that is not by any means the case. It just feels that way. You can't help your emotions, however you can assist what you do with them. Use them emphatically. Try not to permit your distress to overpower you. Concentrate on the constructive parts of these encounters: she is turning into a free individual; she is discovering her own personality; she is longing for having an existence she could call her own, of having any kind of effect on the planet; she is discovering her motivation and building up herself in the public arena. Aren't these the very things you brought her up to do? Isn't this the individual you needed her to turn into? Have you done your occupation well? Yes. Bravo! Furthermore, bravo!

This agony will pass. It's a piece of the child rearing procedure and in that capacity, has its place in your lifespan - yet it's not until the end of time. The day will come when your child will start to demonstrate to you appreciation for all your speculation. You may not get all the commendation and acknowledgment you think you merit, yet you are not searching for that - right? You are searching for the delight of realizing that you had impact in making her what she is today. That is your prize. That is the place the satisfaction is. However, she will bring you what she can by method for thanks and acknowledgment as and when it strikes her.

She may offer you an embrace when you wouldn't dare hoping anymore. She may request that you go to the films with her one day. She may call you while she's sat sitting tight for a train just to say 'hi'. She may post a remark on Facebook telling the world how awesome she supposes you are. She may inquire as to whether you'd like to quite recently hang out one night. She will have her method for revealing to you the amount she adores and admires you yet it won't essentially be your direction. Get it for everything it has - benevolently.

It might be years before she returns to you with the sort of love you feel you require from her. She might never return to you with it. She might basically pour it all on others. What makes a difference is that you realize that the natural product she is bearing in her life is, to a substantial degree, because of you and the affection you have poured on her. Let that be your explanation behind grinning. Let that be your prize. Request nothing from her - she owes you nothing. Yet perhaps, as a result of you, she will carry on with an intentional life; one that bears the product of somebody who had an adoring guardian. Now is the right time to relinquish her now with the goal that she can completely bloom into the individual you have wanted her to be all her life - when she was a 2 year old playing around your feet; when she was a 4 year old on her first day at school; when she was a 8 year old returning home to reveal to you gladly her school venture; when she was a 10 year old letting you know what she needs to be the point at which she grows up; when she was a 12 year old staying over getting it done companion's home for the night; when she was a 14 year old crying on your shoulder in light of the fact that she had dropped out with her closest companion; when she was a 16 year old going to her graduation party; when she was a 18 year old praising her first day as a grown-up. Yes, your occupation is verging on done. Time to give up so she can develop.

CHAPTER TWO: EARLY CHILDHOOD: PREPARING THE NEXT GENERATION

Teaching your children differences between Morality and Ethics

Both ethics and ethical quality help is in noting the inquiry: What would it be advisable for me to do?

We are confronted with this question constantly. Over and over again we settle on vital choices without sufficiently giving time or procedure to coming to the best reply. Why not? Frequently we basically don't know how to settle on such choices. At times we disregard them and trust they will go away, here and there we take after the counsel of others, now and then we simply figure.

On the off chance that we wish to be in charge of our own future and our own choices we ought to invest a little energy thinking and attempting to settle on a decent choice, a superior choice than just picking the least demanding answer.

All in all, ethics and profound quality help us in noting the inquiry: What would it be a good idea for me to do?

Do they give the same answer? No.

Which is the better approach and why?

What is the distinction in the middle of profound quality and ethics?

Huge numbers of us befuddle ethics and ethical quality, numerous individuals use them reciprocally. Be that as it may, they are, altogether different, related however distinctive. The distinction is vital when settling on critical choices, notwithstanding choosing whether you are confronting an ethical problem or a moral issue. Critical when examining such well known themes as religion, sexuality, great and awful, set in stone. Thus, take a couple of minutes now to better comprehend the distinction in the middle of profound quality and ethics.

Kindly, don't allude to the word reference. Word references endeavor to catch well known use and a lot of prevalent utilization of ethics and ethical quality is extremely obscured. Here I can demonstrate to you proper methodologies to utilize every word unequivocally, and make these words as sharp instruments to slice through some really muddled thoughts.

Ethical quality

Ethical quality is a situated of guidelines or rules by which we carry on. Basic? Yes, extremely basic yet the suggestions are critical.

Ethics answer issues we confront in life. Ethics are composed down; they're characterized responses to characterized issues. Illustrations that ring a bell are: Stealing is improper. Infidelity is shameless. Executing someone else is indecent. Fetus removal is shameless. Homosexuality is unethical. Blazing the Christian Bible is improper.

Presently you must admire that somebody must choose these guidelines or rules. On account of the Bible's Ten Commandments that were passed on from the Mount a huge number of years prior, these tenets were talked and composed by the Christian God and afterward potentially translated and deciphered by Moses. When in doubt, ethical quality is controlled by others and took after by individuals who offer certain qualities.

The Ten Commandments were a situated of ten standards which characterized the conduct of a gathering of individuals numerous years back. The principles were viable in that they reverted the Ten Commandments into handy laws and a social structure which characterized an individuals. They gave solidness and gave the premise to a progressing character and advancement.

The way that profound quality gives soundness is a vital and effective part of profound quality. At the point when nature changes, when the old pioneers and tutors pass on, profound quality empowers their qualities, their tenets to proceed. So individuals have solidness. An adjustment in initiative does not mean everybody must begin once more. Individuals feel and are more secure when things are stable. Change and instability are fairly startling. Profound quality gives a premise to an ameliorating strength.

"Thou shalt not desire thy neighbor's home, thou shalt not want thy neighbor's wife" is my review of (a piece of) one of the Ten Commandments. A great many people would concur that it is bad to attempt to lure your neighbor's wife (which may be the outcome on the off chance that you fancy her enough). Indeed, even today it would bring about some really dreadful results if everybody went around alluring one another's wife right, left and focus. It could harm the general public considerably. So that is a really helpful tenet to apply inside most social orders then and today.

In synopsis, ethical quality is a situated of regular values that give steadiness to social orders and separate between social orders.

Ethics

Ethics is a methodology, a technique for deciding. Ethics is about choosing to the best of our capacity, without apprehension or support. It is about being mindful of the numerous parts of every issue and attempting to incorporate them into the choice making procedure. It is about being mindful of the result of our choices, great and terrible.

Ethics is about making an all around considered choice and having the ethical mettle to acknowledge the obligation of our choice.

Ethics is more a method for drawing nearer choices, ethics is not a situated of qualities but rather a method for creating qualities for a certain circumstance as it is caught on.

Do you perceive how it varies from ethical quality? Profound quality is a situated of qualities that are connected, ethics is an approach to settle something at we comprehend it. Ethics can create ethics and as the circumstance changes ethics can advance ethics.

Give us a chance to simply come back to ethics for the time being and I should say all the more in regards to the qualities and shortcomings of every in more detail further on.

Ethics is a method for coming to an answer in any circumstance. The point is to achieve the best reply. However, all issues are muddled. The more we find out around an issue, the more convoluted it gets to be.

Give us a chance to take a basic case. Basic ethical quality states "Thou should not kill someone else." A medication crazed executioner has shot twelve understudies in a classroom and is efficiently shooting more understudies, one at regular intervals. You are arranged behind him ten meters away. You have a weapon and an unmistakable shot at him. Do you shoot and murder him?

Ethical quality says no.

Ethics lets us know we ought to consider the potential result of our choice, how it will influence others and how it influences the world we live in. Ethics instructs us to settle on a choice based upon what we believe is ideal for everything and everybody.

My own particular take is:

- Try not to choose for your own particular advantage, choose for the advantage of others.

- Make the best choice, the most delightful thing.
- Be mindful of the results. To a limited extent they are our obligation.

Do we slaughter him? There is no impeccable set in stone reply here. We must settle on our own choice and live with the results. In the event that we have done as such, then the choice was moral.

Based upon my comprehension of the circumstance, I would shoot to slaughter in light of the fact that it is to the greatest advantage of the remaining understudies. It may have an awful result for me, yet I am less imperative than the understudies. I would judge all the more great would come about because of my slaughtering him.

This is settling on a moral choice.

Nonetheless, perhaps there is something I didn't have the foggiest idea. Possibly it was a film being shot and I for reasons unknown, was ignorant that everybody was acting. Sounds really imbecilic, yet such things happen.

The Problems of Morality and Ethics

Ethical quality gives answers. Profound quality gives arrangements. Ethics are correct, supreme and certain. We can be sure that on the off chance that we choose based upon ethical quality, it is an answer and right based upon the ethical quality. Ethics are helpful and simple. Few inquiries are obliged, believing is constrained, and we take after the standards.

This is an extraordinary quality and a shortcoming. Profound quality gives smart responses to numerous normal choices.

There are such a large number of choices we have to make every day, we can't invest hours on each of them. This is the place profound quality is solid. We can take after our ethics with a reasonable level of certainty on the grounds that in the past they have given a decent result. Ethics are helpful and simple.

Be that as it may, things change. How do the Ten Commandments handle the web? Hereditary designing? Contamination? Atomic force? A worldwide temperature alteration? The Ten Commandments don't have a response for these inquiries on the grounds that the inquiries did not exist or were not asked around then.

Plainly choice making must develop to adjust to current circumstances. However, ethical quality is described by soundness, by outright guidelines. Shouldn't something be said about ethics? Ethics is the area of changed condition. Ethics is liquid and versatile.

Ethics can demonstrate to us best practices to advance our ethics, how to settle on choices in new circumstances.

Ethics is better for the dubious choices, ethical quality is more effective for the general issues we confront every day. Be that as it may, be mindful, don't get smug, profound quality does not question and we frequently need to comprehend and inquiry the purposes for even basic looking issues before settling on a choice. Fare thee well utilizing profound quality, ask yourself is the answer clear or do I have to comprehend somewhat more?

Give us a chance to utilize a straightforward case. The profound quality "Thou should not murder someone else" appears to be direct.

Take a more perplexing illustration inside of the setting of war. Envision airplane pilots shooting regular folks in light of the fact that they looked like purported unsafe agitators. Such choices were made morally in their perspective, they were settling on a choice for the best enthusiasm of different gatherings at some danger to themselves. In insight into the past they may have been off-base, yet the choice can well be called moral. It could similarly be called good in light of the fact that the pilots were taking after the principles.

Profound quality is applying foreordained qualities (generally grew by others) and intended for diverse issues, distinctive predicaments at an alternate time and after that not tolerating the obligation of that choice. "I did it on the grounds that the tenet said as much." This in my perspective is taking the simple alternative, annulling obligation as a rule.

Ethics is applying your qualities to an issue now and settling on the best choice conceivable based upon the accessible data. Such choices turn into your choice and you are in charge of the choice and result partially. Ethics is described by uncertainty, unanswered inquiries and realizing that we can just settle on our best choices and that such choices are not the best for everybody. Each choice has costs and costs are not shared just as. So ethics does not answer the inquiry what is correct or wrong, however what is perhaps better or more regrettable based upon what is known.

Moral choices give conviction, a measure of nobility. Be that as it may, obviously on the grounds that every general public has diverse ethical quality, every general public will settle on contrasting good choices sometimes. Infrequently this is sufficient to produce real clashes regardless of apparently verging on irrelevant contrasts. The way that religion is a central point in clash shows this. The profound quality of every religion is diverse and total. Outright contrasts are hopeless, and create narrow mindedness.

Moral choices give vulnerability and uncertainty. Regardless of the possibility that social orders have varying qualities, taking a moral methodology grants diverse arrangements and an acknowledgement that maybe my choice is not the best for all. This incites a tolerant society, one which takes an all the more "incline toward toleration" approach. Uncertainty is great in that is energizes resilience.

Ethicists are wracked with uncertainty. Moralists are outright in their feelings. Locate a self-satisfied government official and you have discovered an ethical legislator. Locate a tormented government official and you have discovered a more moral lawmaker.

I will close with another sample of where today's general public has an ethical worth which is inconsistent with moral choice making.

Killing. Under the same good code that states we might not kill, society today requests we keep up the life of matured harmed individuals who no more have any craving to live. Our profound quality requests we keep their hearts pulsating, their lungs pumping, utilizing all that current prescription can offer. Ethics asks the inquiry for what reason we ought to keep up the life in this falling flat body propped up by innovation. What is the great that originates from locking out the soul harvester somewhat more? Nobody wishes to endure lastly pass on ever so gradually, bringing on sorrow to their friends and family.

Yet society compels this ethical quality onto every one of us.

I make the inquiry on who picks up from this? Look profound into your heart and think for a minute, think morally. I think that a few individuals pick up by saying "We did whatever we could to keep him alive." This is a method for advocating an unscrupulous choice. A method for staying away from feedback and fault. Being moral is tolerating the outcomes for settling on the best choices.

Keep in mind ethical quality is about repealing obligation? The withering individual settles on their choice and wishes to kick the bucket. For our own egotistical reasons, not for their advantage, another person chooses they must keep on suffering and others must endure so they can be moral.

Killing is moral in the dominant part of cases, however it is improper in many social orders today. Government officials are to a great extent being untrustworthy by permitting this to proceed. They are acting to their greatest advantage - their sense of self expels their moral part from their activities.

Thus, I trust you now comprehend the contrast in the middle of ethics and ethics. It won't change the world tomorrow, nor if it, however in the event that maybe you can simply take somewhat more time to consider imperative choices in moral terms in future then your reality will be a superior, more tolerant spot.

In the event that you need to practice straight away, put forth what are the moral inquiries connected with smoking, with child rearing and garbage sustenance, PC diversions or boxing. What might be said about strolling over the street securely on a Don't Walk sign, constraining children to go to classes where they are problematic in class, smoking a cigarette, working for a liquor or uranium mining organization. What are the ethics of working for a hall gathering, being a government official or a veggie lover?

What's more, review once more, there is no totally right or wrong reply. There are better or more awful replies, yes. Be that as it may, not right or off-base. All the better you can improve comprehend the issues, the outcomes, and who and what is influenced before choosing. You can't settle on a really morally choice until you are on the spot. Furthermore, each moral choice won't be idealize nor please everybody, nor will it be legitimate always, the answer may change tomorrow, however such choices will be yours and the best you can set aside a few minutes with the data you have.

Keep in mind:

Try not to choose for your own particular advantage, choose for the advantage of others.

Make the best choice, the most pleasant thing.

Be mindful of the results. To some extent they are our obligation.

Being moral is extreme, exceptionally intense. However, I know of no better approach to make my decisions. Improve approach to settle on your choices?

Nurturing a relationship with my children from the beginning

Momentum scrutinize in the fields of emotional well-being, mind health and child advancement bolsters the hypothesis that demonstrations of viciousness against a child, regardless of how short or how mellow harms the guardian/child relationship as well as devastates a child's pride and self-regard. Both are connected with a critical increment in a child's powerlessness to child sexual ill-use.

The brutal in all actuality our child rearing decisions will essentially affect on our children's capacity to feel pride in themselves and to completely confide in us. Smacking not just harms the valuable relationship we have with our children, it wrecks their pride and self regard - key qualities they will require to outflank the methodologies of a pedophile and to know they have the trust and acknowledgement of friends and family to trust in the event that they are ever drawn closer thusly. Moreover a child who is strong and creative, who has been raised with affection, regard and given sound limits yet is not lead bound will have the self-regard and mindfulness to perceive and keep away from the methodologies of a pedophile in any case.

The initial phase in this procedure is to see totally that our children need to co-work and speak with us. They would prefer not to disappoint us and to recognize that they are doing the absolute best they can at any given time. When we completely accept this announcement, we can start to change the way we train our children and see their conduct as an intends to express a need, not to just bother, disappoint or outrage us.

The other thing we have to comprehend is that discipline and dangers don't show children how to act in an unexpected way, nor does it propel them to be the best individuals they can be.

Train basically intends to instruct, not to rebuff. Advancing flexibility with solid limits that energizes self-control, obligation, regard for the emotions of others and positive enthusiastic wellbeing ought to be the objective of any lesson with a disciplinary message. Child rearing is about impacting our children through affection and comprehension.

It is likewise essential to recollect, that our children can't "make" us furious or "push our catches" on the off chance that we deliberately decide to stay quiet and in control of our own feelings. It is the point at which a child's conduct is taken actually, that we respond from a position of trepidation and the need to control. Frequently our reactionary position as parents is basically telling the child, 'You have to quit acting thusly so I'll quit feeling along these lines.' Look for these oblivious examples keeping in mind the end goal to quit moving the accuse onto your child for your own responses.

The four components that ought to be dodged when restraining children are:

1) Dread

2) Disgrace

3) Danger

4) Segregation

The accompanying are a couple of thoughts of how to show children conduct, standards, appreciation and wellbeing without depending on smacking, time out or forcing results.

Simply recall that the GOLDEN RULE likewise applies to children, so treat them the way you would be dealt with in ALL ways.

1) Build up structure and routine - Establishing schedule, custom, structure and request into our children's lives in unobtrusive and minding ways is a gentler, less antagonistic method for

conveying teach and appreciation to a home.

2) Hear you out children - The most ideal approach to comprehend you children is to hear them out. Children will usually, impart through their practices, not through their words. So as a guardian, you must look past the conduct to hear the genuine messages they are attempting to express.

3) Work to comprehend your child - Understanding makes trust and collaboration; misconception makes trepidation, disappointment and outrage. When we comprehend our child's reasons for alarm, we are more ready to perceive the association of these apprehensions to

her conduct and more engaged to react with adoration as opposed to responding out of trepidation.

4) It is fantastically enabling to stay in a position of affection amid behavioral upheavals. When we lose control of ourselves, we have adequately lost control of the circumstance and our capacity to decidedly impact our child. Keep in mind that conduct adjustment procedures (evacuation of benefits, establishing, point graphs, and so on.) don't address the hidden anxiety; and in this way, won't instruct your child to figure out how to control when pushed in future circumstances

5) Be sensible in your desires - By having a comprehension of a child's ages and stages we can abstain from setting unreasonable desires on them which can bring about clash and harm trust.

6) Energize innovative articulation of troublesome feelings through craftsmanship, music, development and composing - Children regularly find that through these imaginative exercises, they find themselves able to express things they will be unable to express in words. Try different things with these things with your children. You may even find that a decent sing and move to the Wiggles will cool your fatigued nerves moreover.

7) For conduct that is reoccurring or steady - Look for triggers that may pave the way to the undesirable conduct and when you see the trigger you can expect, intercede, occupy or redirect, before the undesirable conduct happens. As a guardian, take a gander at your child's conduct, however take a gander at what activating occasion brought about the conduct; this perception will prompt understanding and positive arrangements.

8) Be a decent sample yourself - The main intelligent approach to show children about tenets, conduct, appreciation and security is to be a decent illustration yourself. Children do what you do, not so much what you say.

9) Be cool and reliable . Consistency makes a soothing and predicable world for your children and helps them to realize what's in store and what is anticipated from them. They likewise feel safe that you are unsurprising. You say what you mean, mean what you say, and do what you say you are going to do.

10) See troublesome times as open doors for creating critical thinking aptitudes and self-control - for you and your children.

11) Support self-restraint - The most ideal approach to do this by being a positive good example to your children. Model self-restraint by controlling your own particular irate and damaging sentiments and practices. Deal with your own

particular wellbeing, practice and eat solid sustenances and endeavor consistently to be all the things that you wish for your children in all parts of your life.

Give all that you do 100% and endeavor to be the best individual you can be and your children will take action accordingly. Life is a stunning enterprise and to just give it 5% of your exertion is a horrendous waste. Self-control is such a vital fixing in an effective, flexible and glad life. Educate your children about positive self talk and include them in the choice making of family life. Reveal to them how much their data is esteemed and regarded and that you hold their assessments, thoughts and choices on equivalent balance to your own.

A "decent child", bound by standards and disallowances about what his parents need him not to do and who is rebuffed in the event that he neglects to meet these desires, is being denied the chance to support his own particular adaptability, his feeling of force and his own genius. A child taught to take after the standards as opposed to being taught to react instinctively and adaptably to genuine living, continuous data will be at a particular drawback if went up against by the ingenious and unsafe pedophile or molester.

At the point when children feel esteemed and regarded, they are more inclined to tell somebody they trust on the off chance that they are concerned or have endured misuse. Moreover, when they are enabled, they are more prone to be self-assured and self-assured and

less inclined to be focused by potential abusers.

CHAPTER THREE: TOWARDS GOOD GRADES

It is once said that coming to an objective may even be less difficult and less confounded than to look after one. When a man has the capacity reach or clutch an accomplishment, the following step is to keep up the level of execution. It is watched that understudies in secondary school and sophomore years are messed with keeping up the grades they have accomplished in the first quarters or semesters. It is without a doubt conceivable, however, to keep up the execution level to stay safe. Numerous understudies are also mindful of the dropping grades amid the second semester because of the absence of obligation and the trouble of themes adapted as the new semester starts. Nonetheless, every issue has its answer.

Begin off Slow and Sure

It is critical to begin off another school year new yet moderate. Numerous understudies speed themselves up and bring their grades up in the start of the new school year. More than 50% of the understudies however, have their grades dropped because of fatigue, the sudden increment of the level of trouble of an a lot of subjects, and the absence of obligation. It is accordingly, key to begin of moderate yet beyond any doubt. The length of an understudy listens to addresses and takes part in class talks, the likelihood of coming to mid-reach grades is high. The normal execution and the ability of every understudy are totally distinctive. Consequently, the measure of grade an understudy gets will likewise rely on upon one's own qualities. For example, an understudy whose grade point normal reaches from 3.20 to 3.50 is beginning a first year. Since it is a year of secondary school's starting, an understudy would need to go ease back to start with to watch the level of contrast between center school and secondary school. It is critical however, to be mindful of all assignments and addresses gave in classes. Notwithstanding, don't worry and lose control because of the distinctions in secondary school in light of the fact that that can annihilate the whole year.

Utilize the Turtle's Principle in the Race

Numerous ought to be acquainted with the anecdote about the rabbit and the turtle's race. The triumph has a place with the turtle as it gradually moves itself towards the completing line. Not at all like the rabbit, its capacity to run quicker towards the completing line is an outright actuality. The turtle however, won the race on the grounds that it has never halted itself from moving towards the objective.

Understudies as well, ought to utilize this rule to keep up good grades. The rabbit moves speedier than the turtle and the reality itself are pleasing. Be that as it may, if understudies begin off pretty much as the rabbit did, large portions of them will wind up resting in the very end. The absence of obligation and expanding weariness will bring about negative results and terrible grades.

Getting good grades and making scholastic progress is fundamental in life as it decides our future to an extensive degree. Businesses take a gander at our grades and focus our paycheck. Our grades focus the sort of occupations that we do. So how to get good grades? Goodness, you simply must be persevering, listen in class, and get your work done (sounds natural?). That is only the misleading statement. Who doesn't know how to do those? It's simply that the minute I open up my reading material, I feel dormant and lethargic. I simply retain a lump of stuffs. Stay with me here as I manual for make scholastic progress.

Step by step instructions to get good grades

You got the chance to discover your inspiration. Take a seat unobtrusively and think. What is your inspiration for needing to make scholastic progress? What is a definitive objective that you need to accomplish? Do you have an objective that you can work towards it? You got the chance to discover your inspiration before setting your attitude right on needing to get good grades. Be it getting qualifications in your exams with the goal that you can make your parents pleased, or needing to be fruitful in school so that next time you can drive a Ferrari. As I've generally said, inspiration is the best medication. Mulling over can be intense at times, yet inspiration will give you the adrenaline surge and keep you going. That is the thing that separate the good understudies from the normal ones. They realize what they need.

Consider painstakingly the environment that you decide to study in. Is it an uproarious with incidental creature trucks driving pass and bringing your contemplations away? Pick a study domain that is favorable yet not very agreeable to make you tired. I generally like to go to the library to study as the temperature there is only pleasant with a tranquil situation that will help you concentrate on what you're doing.

Arrange your notes and books. When you're compose, an a piece of your cerebrum is arranged for to focus on things that you need to core interest. Record your notes in a document and arrange them into distinctive subjects.

Thusly, it will make it simpler for you to discover your notes when you're changing.

Set away all types of diversions. This may be platitude, yet it works ponders. Securing diversions like your cell telephones and iPod (yes, don't listen to music while contemplating) will augment the time you designate for concentrating on. Getting good grades is knowing how to study effectively. Allotting 2 hours for correction and wind up utilizing your cell telephone to message your companions isn't the most intelligent of thoughts.

CHAPTER FOUR: DIFFERENT PARENTING STYLES - THEIR EFFECTS ON CHILDREN

Parenting styles are typically discussed as far as authoritarian parenting, authoritative parenting, and permissive parenting. What impacts does everyone have on the children getting the parenting? How distinctive will a child be when presented to diverse parenting styles? What's more, which is the right and best parenting style to utilize?

Studies have shown that children who have encountered authoritarian parenting with strict parents frequently aren't ready to think for themselves or comprehend why certain practices are needed. This would bode well as they are raised to do things without addressing them. This is just about the immediate inverse of permissive parenting routines. Children with authoritarian parents are regularly withdrawn or on edge and with low self regard levels. Young men can likewise show outrage and disobedience as they get more established. Authoritative parenting prompts these qualities significantly less frequently.

Permissive parenting, regularly known as "liberal" parenting, has been indicated to prompt youthful, indiscreet conduct, with a slant towards defiance and insubordination. Young men of permissive parents are regularly prone to be low achievers, positively less so than children presented to an authoritative parenting style, furthermore less so than children of the authoritarian parenting strategy. Young men are regularly less self persuaded than young ladies regarding instruction, which adds weight to the connection between liberal parenting and low accomplishment.

Investigations of authoritative parenting have demonstrated that children presented to this "law based" parenting style are the best balanced. Whilst authoritarian parenting can frequently prompt contrasts in conduct in the middle of young men and young ladies, children of authoritative parents show less contrasts in conduct between the sexes. They have a tendency to accomplish higher grades in school, be more useful around the home, and have less social issues. Whilst the contrasts between strict parenting and authoritative parenting are apparent, there are additionally contrasts between the children presented to permissive parenting and the children in this gathering.

Whatever your guardian style, all that you do will somehow influence your child. Whilst it is improbable that any parents will fall conveniently into any of the classes, it is clear from studies and reports that the authoritative parenting style is the best. Authoritarian parenting is frequently thought to be brutal and tormenting and permissive parenting doesn't give children the casings and limits they require. In the event that you cherish your children and consider how your activities shape their future then you are prone to be doing OK.

For the lion's share of mankind's history, parenting was an instinctive procedure, however in the current world parents need to know how to parent. Numerous individuals' methodology parenting the same way they approach school and vocations: with a manual. This has made child improvement and brain research a lucrative recorded, as prove by the ceaseless arrangements of parenting books and sites. We need to know how to parent, yet we need somebody to let us know how.

Since parenting methodologies and child improvement got to be well known in the 1940's when Dr. Benjamin Spock presented his fundamental work Baby and Child Care, there have been a heap of techniques advanced for best raising your offspring. Notwithstanding, in the course of recent years, numerous child clinicians now concur that parenting styles can be come down to three gatherings: Authoritarian, authoritative, and permissive. We should investigate the attributes of these parenting system with a specific end goal to show signs of improvement thought of how to parent and the styles that are out there:

Authoritative/law based: Authoritative parents are about equalization: they are occupied with creating composed, persevering, knowledgeable children. Be that as it may, they likewise need to verify their children get some pleasure out of their lives notwithstanding figuring out how to be organized and very much acted. Authoritative parents quality consolidating control and limits with adoration and warmth. They esteem their children's sentiments and info yet are a definitive leaders.

They are not their children's companions but rather they are not their children's bosses either.

Permissive parents: Permissive parents let their children sit in the driver's seat. They feel as if all individuals from the family are measure up to and don't prefer to make a progression of power. Permissive parents feel that children can settle on their own decision and they make an effort not to meddle by setting up structures of order or limits. They need their children to grow up with a high-feeling of self-regard and self-esteem, and they feel that brutal discipline meddles with this procedure.

Authoritarian parents: Authoritarian parent's utilization train and structure to make an effective family unit, and an authoritarian family is not a vote based system: children basically do as they are told. An extremely strict, clear arrangement of principles and regulations run the authoritarian home and these sorts of parents accept that children can just develop appropriately when firmly controlled.

So which of the parenting styles above is the right one? That all relies on upon what you look like at life, however numerous child analysts concur that authoritative parenting creates the healthiest children on the grounds that it is about making parity. Children should be cherished, listened, and reflected so as to grow up with an in place self-esteem and general feeling of self, however they additionally require limits and teach to learn compassion and that the world doesn't rotate around them. Permissive parenting focuses a lot on creating self-esteem and distinction, and authoritarian parenting focuses a lot on order, and both of these techniques can really prompt low self-regard. It is at last up to you to choose how to parent, yet picking the authoritative style is likely your most solid option.

- **Authoritarian** - This style of parenting guarantees that the guardian is in control. Parents will endeavor to apply control over the child. Children will be given no decisions and no motivation behind why things isn't possible other than how the guardian needs it done. There are normally strict principles that are upheld and if the child does not hold fast to these tenets, they will be brutally rebuffed. Parents who parent thusly are regularly reproachful of their children and will concentrate on awful conduct as opposed to good. Parents who hone an authoritarian style of parenting are by and large not responsive or tender with their children. These children will frequently experience issues thinking for themselves; will have lower self-regard and will probably not be as glad as children brought up in an alternate parenting style.

- **Permissive** - The permissive guardian gives complete control over to the child. They will have few principles, less schedules and likely couple of limits, if any. Their parenting style is conflicting in light of the fact that they don't finish on anything. Their children will have numerous decisions, and regularly ones that are conflicting with their ages. They are liberal parents who would prefer not to get included in debate with their children. Thus there is little teach. These sorts of parents have a tendency to be warm and adoring and want to be their child's companion as opposed to a guardian. Children raised by permissive parents are frequently not cheerful, may perform ineffectively in school and may have issues with power figures.

- **Democratic** - The vote based guardian will help their children figure out how to be dependable; to consider the results of their conduct; will have sensible desires for their children and will screen their conduct. These parents concentrate on good conduct and if poor conduct is shown, a superior method for doing something is disclosed or indicated to the child instead of brutally rebuffing them. Decisions are given to the child with respect to their age. These parents are warm and adoring and realize that for good parenting to be viable a bond must be built up in the middle of guardian and child. This style of parenting creates the best results with more content and more fruitful children.

A fourth, yet not as normal style of parenting is the **Uninvolved Parent**. This guardian makes few requests on the child and will have restricted correspondence with them. These parents will have a tendency to lead experience that are full and finish yet truly isolate from their children. The children's essential needs are met however they get little warmth and supporting. These children will have less self-regard and be less equipped than children raised with different styles of parenting.

In light of the diverse parenting styles, and on the grounds that every individual decides their parenting style in view of different circumstances, a potential issue can emerge when individual parents every have their own particular totally distinctive styles of parenting. This won't just cause disarray with the children however can add to issues in settling on common choices when raising a gang.

Albeit parenting can be one of the hardest employments there are, it can likewise be a standout amongst the most fulfilling. On the off chance that we can approach parenting utilizing a parenting style that is liable to be the best in bringing up glad and fruitful children, we will harvest the prizes in later years, thus will our children.

The Drawbacks of Permissive Parenting

Permissive parenting implies that parents let their children do whatever they need. These sorts of parents would prefer not to put in any work in forming their child's future. Once in a while, this sort of parenting style is a consequence of the strict childhood the parents themselves probably had. In any case, permissiveness can be exceptionally harming if the guardian does not check when the child is doing something incorrectly.

Much the same as the authoritative sort of guardian, a permissive guardian is frightened. For this situation, the guardian believes that in the event that they put an excess of limitations on their child, the child will detest them. There is not at all like that in actuality really. This could be the outcome where the guardian was raised in a strict set up and they figured out how to aversion their own particular parents. She or he may have regard for their own parents, however no adoration. They fear the same situation would rehash with their children.

Permissive parenting is careless furthermore an awful method for raising children. The parents can run over is languid and laid back. All in all, children who have such parents need certainty and focused soul.

Parents, who are permissive, support all the wrong sorts of behavioral examples in the child. The children don't take after tenets and they think that it hard to comply with others' standards when they grow up. They additionally wind up being gotten rowdy or insubordinate children in the school. Kids who have been raised with this sort of parenting are off guard socially. What's more, these children would even be considered socially disabled.

Permissive parenting is one of the sorts of parenting styles wherein the guardian and the child normally get along together. Nonetheless, there are generally insignificant behavioral desires set for the child. There is likewise ordinarily no obviously characterized arrangement of standards so the child is allowed to do whatever he or she needs. Some say that permissive parenting can be useful for the child in the advancement of experimentation and investigation. It has a few disadvantages.

Parents, who have exceptionally occupied calendars, may have a tendency to have a permissive parenting style. Occupied parents styles of decision are frequently at the edges of the scope of styles. These parents, having little time to manage their children, permit a flexibility of practices, with few if any breaking points, on their children. Children may get those things they need or particularly request. This may be because of keeping the peace in the family unit.

The children in these family units may be adverse influenced in their advancement of social and group aptitudes. Children feel much more secure with predictable age proper cutoff points and limits. In this protected environment, they have a tendency to get the consideration, adoration, and direction that they particularly require in their developmental years. Permissive parenting may be rehearsed by parents who had a strict childhood and in a yearning to present the inverse environment to their children. There is a contrast between openness to investigation and permissiveness.

The general ramifications are that permissive parents may confront the consequences of turning out to be unreasonably merciful with conduct. Conduct impediments are proposed to educate the children how to sum up known breaking points to self-protection and self-inspiration. Some permissive parents offer into fits just so that the difficulty of the fit of rage closures. Some likewise sense a fit and offer into evade the fit of rage through and through. This activity really educates the child to utilize fits of rage to control the responses of their parents.

A portion of the qualities of children who have been raised by unnecessarily permissive parenting are frequently adolescence, powerlessness to control driving forces, an absence of center, and failure to acknowledge obligation. As grown-ups, these children could likewise think that it difficult to act naturally adequate or mindfully free.

It is essential to find all the data about permissive parenting. Clearly, I have spoken to a fairly negative perspective of permissive parenting. It has downsides. You will need to peruse all the more about any beneficial outcomes that are available with utilization of this style of parenting. I solidly accept that it is each parent's, inside of the family structure and objectives, alternative and obligation to pick scrupulously how the family will be organized. With the goal children should go into the universe of today also adjusted people, show them how to pick their own behavior, values, and aptitudes, and acknowledge the constructive or antagonistic outcomes of their activities.

You can hunt down more data about permissive parenting on the web, through some parenting care groups, or your neighborhood bookkeeper will be upbeat to help you in discovering more printed material on the subject. To Your Parenting Success

Life is loaded with difficulties for occupied parents, and parenting is a major one. It is safe to say that you are Trying to Save Time with Permissive Parenting? There have been times that we parents have all accomplished the baffling practices of our children. Try not to let this dissatisfaction cause you to dismiss your family objectives. Make your own objectives and parenting arrangement of activity with parenting guiding internet parenting classes. There is worth to expanding and enhancing our parenting aptitude.

CHAPTER FIVE: PARENTING SHY CHILDREN

Alternative Birthday Party Ideas for Shy Children

Not every child has a gaggle of companions. Timid children, particularly, might just have maybe a couple companions with which they feel sheltered and close. Along these lines, welcoming a bundle of colleagues to a birthday gathering may not be exceptionally a good time for the child or the visitors. Here are some option festivity thoughts for the modest child and their closest companion or companions.

Go to the neighborhood entertainment Mecca. Numerous parks permit parents to lease a structure or a forest for an ostensible charge. The parents, perhaps joined by relatives or grown-up companions near to the child, can appreciate a day of amusement while the child and his or her closest companion make their rounds of the rides and attractions. Contingent upon the child's age, the grown-ups can walk the children through the recreation center or just set meet-up times. On the off chance that the children are being let out of the grown-ups' sight, verify they have a grown-up's cell phone number on the off chance that they get to be lost or are gotten by park security for any reason. The telephone ought to be kept an eye on at all times and completely charged.

Look at the zoo. For a child that cherishes creatures, seeing the zoo with a closest companion and a grown-up can be the ideal birthday treat. A lackadaisical walk around the greater part of the displays, closed with supper and a stop at the blessing shop will leave the child with a superior valuation for creatures and environment. Having the capacity to pick their own blessing from the blessing shop is certain to awe! In the event that the grown-up takes photographs of the a few children together, send a duplicate of the best one as a post-festivity support of the exceptional day.

Book a day at the spa. Timid children are regularly just hesitant with their companions! While back rubs or body-wraps may be a lot for young ladies, nail treatments, hair medicines, and pedicures in the casual climate of the spa may be only the thing for a high schooler or teen young lady and her closest companion. A guardian or other same-sexual orientation grown-up may be needed by the spa to go hand in hand with the young ladies. Finish off the day with a delectable pastry and blessings at home.

Having stand out or two nearby companions doesn't need to make a birthday festivity exhausting. Treat the modest child to a day more suited to less individuals and make the most of it! Having a great time at the carnival, zoo, or spa urges the child to be out openly and having a fabulous time, without being confronted with the gazes and overpowering consideration of a conventional gathering.

"Birthdays" are an essential day for the birthday individual. Some of the time it is more than only a birthday on the grounds that it transforms into a colossal family assembling and everybody one is having an extraordinary time.

How to Treat Your Shy Children

Give me a chance to start by saying almost immediately that I don't believe there's anything especially off with being timid. A few individuals are conceived thoughtful people and a few individuals are conceived social butterflies and there is nothing innately good or awful about both of those.

Mentally, it's just an issue of our brains having the capacity to process different signs on the double versus just a couple at once. Those that procedure numerous signs have a tendency to be outgoing and those the procedure few have a tendency to be independent. It has nothing to do with insight or anything like that, it's a basic mechanical procedure similar to multitasking.

That being said there are a few things you can do to help your timid child turn out to be additionally cordial and I think we can all concur that this kind of thing ought to be valuable to your child.

Above all else give your child the time that they have to end up OK with a thing. Commonly children aren't timid, they're only a bit anxious or frightened and they require more opportunity to get used to a thing than you may anticipate. Tolerance goes far here and telling them that they have all the time they need can be vital.

Next tell your child that their cooperation in a specific action must be somewhat their choice.

It's staggeringly vital to give your child a decision regarding things like this. Making them feel like they have some control of the circumstance can work ponders and can likewise help them manufacture certainty and permit them to wander forward into new things later on.

Reprimanding your children shyness does not help at all, shape, or frame and can especially harm them in various routes, for example, undermining their self-assurance and making them more averse to attempt new things later on.

That leads us into my next tip which is to not mark your child as withdrawn or timid. In the event that a child dependably hears his parents calling him bashful to himself or to others he or she will begin to trust it regardless of the fact that they aren't really modest. It's regularly simple for parents, particularly when conversing

with different parents to say something like

"goodness he's the modest one in the family" or

something to that effect yet you truly need to

prevent yourself from saying things like that in

light of the fact that it can have a gigantic

negative impact on your child- particularly over

the long run as they keep on listening to these

things for quite a while and a seemingly endless

amount of time.

Five Ways for Parents to Help Their Children to Overcome Shyness

So there you have a few tips and traps is you can

use to handle the conduct of your timid child.

Some of these tips will help push your child into

all the more friendly region yet recall, toward the

day's end that the absolute most renowned individuals in history of the world were mercilessly modest... simply something to remember!

Shyness does not have an institutionalized definition in the lexicon and can't be characterized by maybe a couple words. Constrained, alarmed, bashful are only a couple. Most definitions fuse feeling uncomfortable in social circumstances. The straightforward demonstration of perceiving and comprehension a child's emotions can make a domain that feels sheltered or more secure to a bashful child.

Fifty percent of the grown-up populace in the United States is bashful. The vast majority are humiliated by their shyness and keep it covered up. They some way or another accept they are unique in relation to others. Fusing the accompanying tips will go far to bail bring a timid child out of their shell.

Depict shyness in a positive light: Compare your bashful child to other modest children who have grown up to be fruitful grown-ups. Case in point: Abraham Lincoln was greatly bashful as a kid and was perplexed about young ladies. Indeed, even motion picture stars like Tom Hanks were agonizingly modest. Clarify that bashful individuals can be a bigger number of bold than the normal individual. It takes more vitality for a timid individual to do likewise things a cordial individual can do.

Keep correspondence lines open regularly: A timid child will feel closer to the gang. All it takes is a grin, remark or even an inquiry to have a major effect. The key is not to make your child learn about singled and not the same as different children.

Urge a timid child to join an additional curricular movement gathering: Shy children need to feel like they are adding to a reason and they require motivation to communicate with different children their own age.

Compliment them on their achievements openly: Most timid children pine for consideration yet avoid it in the meantime. This is the reason it is vital to be watchful when attracting regard for them. The attempt at manslaughter methodology works best. Try not to give them the time to battle or react. "Awesome sweater. I truly like it. What would I be able to accomplish for you?"

Move forward and realize that you did a good thing.

Remunerate little upgrades: Most timid children bloom when difficulties are broken into sensible lumps. It's their uneasiness that hinders their advancement, not their insight. Numerous bashful children figure out how to defeat their reasons for alarm when it is made clear that falling flat is a piece of learning.

At the point when shyness goes unnoticed or amended, it can have a troubling impact on a grown-up child's life. It is feasible for bashful children to wind up thoughtful grown-ups and pass up a great opportunity for some open doors in life in light of the fact that nobody ever exhibited that shyness can be succeed.

CHAPTER SIX: TEENAGE DELINQUENCY

The Teenage Condition - The Two Headed Monster Explored

Am only in my lamenting for the early childhood of my little girl? I think back to those pink and white grandness days with sentimentality, longing for when she sat before a gathering of dolls or plastic horses, brushing manes and tails and murmuring a tune from the most recent Little Kitty film.

Her room was swathed in cotton sweet pink tulle, huge bows all over; a gathering of powder puffs splendid patches of shading in the daylight separating through chiffon wraps. Where has that sweetheart young lady gone?

She appears to have vanished and been supplanted by a reprobate evil spirit in dark holey tights, wearing a skull and crossbones pendant and wearing a gathering of ceaseless adornments; headphones and cellular telephones. At regular intervals or something like that she returns, reflexive hair prodding against my cheek, generally just before the head vanishes once more, into the icebox.

There was never a room like my girls room. She has gathered the most noticeably awful questions in the house and masterminded them around her space to make it look as terrible as could be allowed. Some place under an untidy heap of clothing there is a brilliant blue carpet with cream blossoms. Some place in her closet there is a clean thing of attire, yet not on a holder.

Shoes have been regarded by her as weird things just worn by self important individuals attempting to be something they are not, obviously. Mentors are worn by typical people, particularly exhausted coaches bearing the stains of unidentified substances trodden through amid a few stone shows.

Blonde hair has been shading washed with a shade some place in the middle of purple and maroon, with glowing qualities in direct daylight for reasons unknown I lean toward not to research. The companions of her chest appear to mirror her own abnormal clique design sense, one young fellow really has his ears not pierced but rather practically torpedoed by these inquisitive jolt like things, which extend the flaps, making the pierced cavity in any event a large portion of an inch in distance across and bringing about spectators to recoil away with sickening dread.

A couple of evenings back she showed up in the kitchen wearing a long dark coat which came to the floor, fishnet tights, a dark small skirt with silver studs down the side, a dark laborer pullover and dark nail shine. She needed to recognize what she ought to wear to a dark witch themed birthday party. She was not really in outfit up 'til now! I recommended she put on a dark frilly lower leg length underskirt over boots and include silver gems. She denied on grounds of my thoughts not being sufficiently ladylike!

Teenagers achieve the age of thirteen with an issue immovably set up called ETP - Exact Teenage Programming. This condition is anything but difficult to overcome giving you watch the accompanying rules.

When you need your teenager to bring utilized glasses, glasses and plates from out of his/her space to the kitchen, recollect to include 'And place them in the dishwasher.' under no circumstances hazard a guideline, for example, 'Bring them upstairs,' as I did one evening and afterward was shocked to discover a gathering of filthy dishes on the top step.

Other eminent expressions, for example, 'would you be able to put some washing in please sweetheart' ought to be qualified with 'ideally a choice of everybody's, not simply your own.'

'Would you be able to take the waste out?' must be the best of all. There are such a large number of purposes of relinquishment between the kitchen and the waste can. Be particular.

Teenagers are unequipped for tossing a void container in the receptacle, yet will walk a further separation to give back the vacant container to the refrigerator, would you be able to clarify that? Continuously tap containers when just half purge, that way you will abstain from listening to the spouse thunder when he grabs a depleted container of juice.

Loo rolls are deliberately expelled from their divider mounted holders in bathrooms and moved over the restroom floor so they disentangle around the room like a sterile trim. I have now obtained one of those Poor Man Dispensers that apportion three sheets at once and lock against further unwinding. They have them in detainment facilities, mental organizations and our home.

I sit tight calmly for the dim one to advance out of the dark teenage stage into the light of adulthood and womanliness. At some point or another my daughter is going to get back home again and when she does I should be holding up.

Parental Delinquency - The Bane of the Modern Day Home

Lately, we just caught wind of "juvenile delinquency" and "parental delinquency" was not even a word. The cutting edge society has gotten a bizarre conduct that can never been clarified, even by the key performing artists themselves. Things are truly escaping from hands and numerous families are at the edge of breakdown.

What has happened today? Is the world flipping around, for sure?

Indeed, gone are those days when parents take up the obligations of showing their children profound quality and the premise of growing up. It is plainly expressed in the Bible that when you require some serious energy to show or instruct a child in transit he ought to go, when he grows up, he'll not withdraw from it, but rather things are no more as some time recently. Today's parents require the training more than the children they bring into the world. In the past days, you can recognize a good or awful family by the practices of the children that leave such families. Today, parents are no more their children's good examples - they disregard their obligations and endow weightier matters under the control of procured hirelings. It is troublesome today to see parents who stay back to invest energy with their children. They leave home as ahead of schedule as 7:00am and decline to return until the children are snoozing during the evening, leaving just the cleaning specialist responsible for the home. How would we expect a child who is denied of parental consideration to be sincerely steady?

In numerous homes, the children don't see or stay with their parents for up to 10 minutes a day, and some of the time they don't see them by any means. When we discuss building a rational and gainful society, we shouldn't commit the error of leaving the primary driver of our inconveniences behind in light of the fact that it will unquestionably not take care of any issue. A few teenagers that were gotten at different areas for furnished theft and improper practices separately advised their captors that they needed to draw in the consideration of their parents, on the grounds that without doing something astounding, their parents will never pay consideration on their desires.

In spite of the fact that juvenile delinquency is a separated issue and teenagers are for the most part awful, however the main thing that is by and large terrible is the general origination. In the event that parental delinquency is not tended to and given genuine consideration, all endeavors of tackling issues that begin from the home-front, particularly teenage behavioral issues will yield no natural products.

What to Do About an Irresponsible Teenager

Teenagers, similar to grown-ups, have distinctive levels of untrustworthiness that can extend from sluggishness about errands to lying (to evade obligation or responsibility) to brutal and/or reprobate conduct. The discriminating inquiries are: what level of flippancy does the teenager illustrate, how constant is the flightiness and are there examples to the untrustworthiness?

Clearly, there are two standards about mediations: one, the early an intercession happens implies a more prominent probability of effectively halting and turning around the practices, and two, the more extended the practices proceed with implies that more prominent intercessions will be expected to change or stop the conduct and/or the more serious the untrustworthy conduct will get to be.

The good news is that numerous teenagers develop out of their unreliability just by maturing. On the other hand, not every single flippant example of conduct have that promising end to present circumstances and the finished result is either imprisonment or treatment programs. Numerous variables can impact the consequent result for the teenager, among them being: his/her scholarly execution, enthusiastic security, family dependability, individual hobbies and objectives, and identity variables.

Sorts of Interventions

Parental Interventions

The least demanding and slightest exorbitant (cash and time) is for parents to intercede and stop the flippant conduct. This may mean realizing what they have been doing to unknowingly strengthen the undesirable practices and/or recognize what empowers the flighty conduct. This level of mediation is most proper for the gentle levels of flightiness: sluggishness, disregarding bearings and/or duties, and so on. This level of conduct may best be served by making a behavioral investigation. This procedure is something parents could do themselves with direction from an educated individual or they could counsel with somebody having those abilities. Another choice is for parents to situated up a contracting framework for conduct administration of the high schooler to compensate his/her suitable practices (or obligations) with acquiring cash in lieu of a stipend; the adolescent would focus his/her own wage in view of execution. Data about these subjects is accessible on the Parent Modules page of the site for Parents Teach Kids. This level of intercession will most like be a piece of the more serious or more term flippant practices however will infrequently roll out any critical improvement all alone.

Master Interventions

The following level of mediation is counseling an advocate or analyst who can go about as a go between the guardian and the teenager. This can be extravagant regarding both cash ($75-125/hour) and time for travel and the arrangements. Some of the time wellbeing protection takes care of these costs, however all insurance agencies contrast on prerequisites and methodology so parents would be all around encouraged to register with their advantages before making the arrangements. Advising could conceivably realize changes and can take quite a while to roll out any improvement by any stretch of the imagination. Joint guiding may be needed, for some parents accidentally contribute fundamentally to their teenagers' reckless practices. Case in point, they may give the teenager a charge card and a recompense and additionally an auto, yet they may not be sure about who will pay the gas bills on the MasterCard or a proper utilization of the card. This level of mediation is additionally prescribed for teenagers who are taking part in dangerous conduct (counting substance utilization and unprotected sex) or who have come into contact with the law and the intelligent outcomes for their activities. This level of intercession will most like be a piece of the more extreme or more term unreliable practices yet will infrequently roll out any huge improvement all alone.

Lawful Interventions

At the point when the teenager's flighty conduct has been long-standing and/or serious, parents will probably have couple of alternatives: detainment or a private treatment system having some expertise in the teenager's unending issues (substance misuse, delinquency, and so on.). Once more, these projects may be secured by wellbeing protection advantages and parents would be astute to counsel the best possible people to focus their advantages and limits, referral procedures, and so forth. The projects outside detainment normally require parental contribution in guiding and/or conduct administration aptitudes preparing.

Concentrate On Positive Potentials

Simply in light of the fact that your teenager doesn't do his/her errands, it doesn't mean (s)he is unreliable. Obligation is a character attribute that accompanies encounters of settling on choices and encountering results for those choices. At the point when parents shield their children from the legitimate results of their conduct, they do an extraordinary shamefulness to the child. The child realizes there is nothing that (s)he can't do as there is no expense to the child. Now and then the best showing instrument is the encounters that results bring. The teenager can possibly be who and what you generally imagined him/her to be. Now and again the whole family needs to become mixed up in battling their way through the obscure, individual apprehensions and missteps to locate the magnificent individual inside. Some take long than others to uncover themselves.

Juvenile Delinquency - Youth Crimes

Wikipedia characterizes Juvenile Delinquency as a solitary and illicit conduct by a youthful or teenager. A term given to juveniles who perpetrate criminal acts. A juvenile in addition is a man less than eighteen years old or the individuals who are still a minor. Regarding the matter of delinquency, a court is dependably include in choosing what age a minor falls, particularly with regards to criminal offenses. Particular systems are available in managing juvenile delinquency regarding the matter of lawfulness, for example, detainment communities for denounced juvenile. These people are not stirred up with those denounced grown-ups. In addition, juvenile delinquency is comparable to Youth unlawful acts, youth wrongdoings is a noteworthy issue these days routinely said in news and others. Besides, juvenile unlawful acts can be a minor one or a more genuine one like homicide or crime. If at any time a juvenile one carries out a wrongdoing, he/she is attempted in a court framework which is altogether different from a grown-up one. On the off chance that demonstrated blameworthy he/she will be sent to a detainment focuses made only for them.

Juvenile courts and judges exist for juvenile delinquency exists. In many examples, juveniles who carry out unlawful acts are attempted under the juvenile court that is more qualified to handle instances of juveniles contrasted with an ordinary court. The case is typically left there in the court for choice of the level of danger the juvenile stance in the general public and additionally the advantages that the juvenile will get in the confinement focus if demonstrated liable. Discovering an option method for restoration for the child is one of the obligations of the juvenile court, this likewise to forestall future issue with the child. Larger part of these cases, when the child achieves the age of eighteen, their unlawful acts are normally wiped out, given that they haven't carried out some other wrongdoings.

Contributing variables that may prompt juvenile delinquency shows up in large number of speculations like nature/ sustain standards, how the child was raised, and his/ her encompassing surroundings while growing up among others. The growing up environment of the child is likewise essential, for instance, is the child a misused child or dismissed by parents.

Other than sustain rule, hereditary qualities has additionally been connected to assume a major part in the improvement of juvenile delinquency, however the majority of the specialists on this field repudiate this association. As indicated by them it can just constitute an inclination toward a certain conduct. Specialists still accepted that nurturance or the absence of it is the principle etiology of the advancement of such condition. Distinguishing the base of child's tricky conduct will help in setting up the sort of treatment for the child, and the child can be given thought concerning their conduct.

In overseeing juvenile delinquency, conceptualizing projects is an extremely prevalent approach in handling the issue. A program that will help the child keep from carrying out future wrongdoings. Regularly, a program that spotlights on averting medication utilize and giving early instruction and help to the child. Notwithstanding the way that society's endeavors to control juvenile delinquency are commendable, it is fundamental to note that they are not generally effective. Notwithstanding, the plain demonstration of evading juvenile delinquency through intercession is superior to simply permitting it to happen.

Concerning parenting adolescents today, you can never have an excess of data and that is precisely what we offer. We have sorted out our articles by point: Teen Health; Education; Troubled Teens; Teen Drug Abuse; Tips For Parenting Teens; and Other Teen Issues. The majority of the articles included on this site have been composed by parents that have picked up experience by raising adolescents they could call their own. The substance contained on this site is offered to people in general as data, encounters, and the viewpoints of different parents.

ParentingTeens.com does not claim to offer any sort of medicinal or helpful exhortation or suggestions. We are cheerful to offer the viewpoints and assessments of different parents however that is all. We urge all parents to offer their feelings and encounters with any of the points on our site. We likewise want to hear what parents of youngsters might like to see on this site. So don't hesitate to contact us via email and let us comprehend what you think about the site or on the off chance that you might want to add to the site.

Are You Fed Up With Your Defiant Teenager?

On the off chance that you are a guardian who has the real situation of a resistant teenager to manage, you are probably, feeling down! You might likewise be feeling overpowered, and far more atrocious yet, similar to there is no trust that things will show signs of improvement. Read along so you can increase some accommodating, valuable, and pragmatic data that exceptionally well may turn your circumstance around!

If your child is a preteen, or early teenager, there may be a few things you need to consider. Furthermore, regardless of the fact that your child has come to the teenage years, these things ought to be considered. They generally need to do with how you teach them.

It is without a doubt the standard to holler or shout at, humiliate, censure, address, disgrace, debilitate or hit your children. Possibly hitting is not in style as much any longer, but rather the other parenting procedures positively are still exceptionally common. The thing is that these are not viable, or others conscious, for some imperative reasons!

Firstly, children, particularly when they are more youthful, just realize what we show them. They are mirrors, or wipes that douse up all that we do. When we adversely drop the hammer on them, we show them to do those exceptionally things.

Furthermore, we are, undoubtedly, attempting to show them a lesson when we parent thusly. The thing is that they close down and don't hear anything we attempt to let them know. They just hear an uproarious or negative voice putting them down.

Thirdly, these negative methods for parenting really, just fuel our insubordinate teenager and their displeasure. At whatever point we cause trepidation and anxiety to raise, something many refer to as cortisol gets delivered in additional sums, and therefore goes to the their cerebrum. The outcomes of this are not good. They are compelled to carry on in light of the fact that they get to be confused. In the long haul, they can get to be delinquents and can have sociopathic practices and inclinations.

When you set up the majority of this together, it is clear that nothing is picked up by utilizing those negative types of child control. You shouldn't thrash yourself in the event that you typically parent in this way, in light of the fact that it is the way the dominant part of us were demonstrated to do things by our own parents. When you include the weights of our quick paced society, and how quick are children grow up, it is a characteristic procedure for us to get disappointed on occasion, and afterward fall back on these old, natural procedures.

Ideally you've been edified a touch about what may have been turning out badly in the middle of you and your disobedient teenager. Presently, all that is left to do is add to some new, positive methods for parenting!

Two Parenting Mistakes With Anxious Children

Tyler starts to cry, raising his hands to cover his eyes. Eleven-year old young men hate to cry, and Tyler is particularly frightful of it. It humiliates him and makes him feel powerless, even inside of the protected environment of my advising room. His mother knows this, and with watery eyes herself connects and rubs his shoulder. "I'm sad, nectar," she says. With that he starts to cry harder, hanging over his crossed legs on the sofa. I ponder internally. One of the two mix-ups parents can make in managing a restless child. In fact, mothers support and solace their stinging children. Yes, obviously. However, is it conceivable with a restless child that may be the altogether wrong thing to do?

North American children are encountering clinical tension at perpetually expanding rates. The National Institute of Mental Health reports that thirteen percent of U.S. children experience confused nervousness, while the figure for grown-ups is twenty-percent. The University of Michigan Depression Center, the country's first and foremost such center, appraises that fifteen percent of understudies across the nation experience the ill effects of tension.

Unmistakably children are enduring uncommon levels of clinical nervousness, discovering their brains commandeered by a horde of apprehensions. Indeed, even the most well intentioned guardian is not instinctively furnished to manage this. As an expert advocate who, for unequivocally a zillion years, has helped on edge children and their parents, I've seen anguished parents flopping to make sense of how to best parent a dreadful child. I have seen generally able and good-intentioned parents incidentally commit errors that really prevent the flexibility of their children. By perceiving and adjusting these two parenting missteps, a guardian can turnaround their child's stresses and set them free.

The primary oversight parents gain in obstructing their children's ground in overcoming nervousness is to feel frustrated about them. A guardian sees their child enduring and it makes them extremely upset. They anticipate onto the child their own particular recollections of affliction and torment, and erroneously accept that the child must be feeling pretty much as terrible. In some cases the child does, however frequently they don't. Restless children sob effectively, and notwithstanding if their tears are discharging strain or, sometimes, controlling the circumstance, the shrewd guardian won't react by feeling frustrated about the child.

Seeing Tyler's tears make mother's day. She needs his tears to stop, so she suspends his development forward towards opportunity and how about we him free. Feeling frustrated about him just energizes Tyler's feeling of defenselessness and misery. He may translate his mother's worry as, "Gee, she supposes I can't deal with it either so I must be truly feeble!" The mutual condition of apprehension by both mother and child makes further reliance. Tyler, accepting he is unequipped for driving forward through enthusiastic push and seeing that affirmed by his mother's reaction, looks for mother's solace perpetually. Mother, misinformed by her conviction that a mother's occupation is to dependably show love and backing for her child by consoling and facilitating his apprehensions, accepts she is a minding mother and doing the right thing. They nourish off one another and the example extends, now and again forever. I've worked with numerous fathers who have attempted to break the mother/child enthusiastic ward bond without much of any result. It's just when mother comprehends the passionate prize she's getting from the relationship, and the cost paid by her child, that she stops to excessively comfort him. Inability to let a child battle sustains the child's defenseless state and prompts the misstep number two.

The second parenting oversight made by parents of on edge children is to safeguard their child from agony. I once worked with two sisters who were startled of frightening films. I'm not talking blood and guts films, but rather Disney motion pictures! Each time the miscreant had their enormous scene, the young ladies requested the motion picture be stop and their parents speedily suited them. They never had watched a Disney film to the end. The young ladies were honing, and the parents were fortifying, the most obvious adapting conduct that both children and grown-ups utilization to manage their reasons for alarm: shirking. The entire family moved far from the apprehension to smooth the young lady's restless reaction, however it just fortified the trepidation over the long haul. I clarified the guardian that in light of the fact that the children never figured out how to endure the alarming parts, they never figured out how to quiet their flight reaction and experience the cheerful completion. I assembled a family conference, clarified the how they all moved the dance of shirking to Disney motion pictures, and gave them new strides to move.

A profoundly successful method used to help children overcome apprehension is called presentation. Introduction is the procedure of presenting the trepidation inciting jolt in a continuous manner and permitting the child to developed resistance to it. Gradually, regulated, the child beats their trepidation through progressive introduction and resistance development. The key segment that empowers this procedure to be effective is the child's eagerness to endure little measurements of anguish. By figuring out how to deal with one's brief conditions of affliction, the child picks up dominance over the on edge creating background. So my solution for these sisters was to go home, have the entire family cuddle up on the love seat, and watch the motion pictures from start to finish through, finding through presentation that they could actually handle the alarming parts and that it all works out at last. It worked and the young ladies can now watch the films all alone.

Juvenile Justice and Delinquency Prevention Reauthorization Act - Giving Youth a Second Chance

What is the hidden justification of state juvenile equity frameworks? Is it to rebuff young people who carry out criminal acts or to restore adolescents to give them another opportunity? Despite the fact that this ceaseless level headed discussion plays out likewise for detained grown-ups, what is interesting to the juvenile detainment examination is the individuals who are most influenced: adolescents. Yes, they should be remedied when they do something incorrectly in any case, would it say it isn't likewise essential to put resources into them and give them the chance to develop and develop into adulthood? At the point when considering components that add to juvenile delinquency, for example, psychological well-being and substance use issues, negative ecological impacts, or convoluted family circumstances, the part of state juvenile equity frameworks and group suppliers turns out to be clear - to forestall juvenile delinquency at whatever point conceivable and to restore adolescents who are in the framework to give them the most obvious opportunity to succeed.

Studies have demonstrated that 70 percent or a greater amount of adolescents who are safely kept in a juvenile equity office have a psychological wellness or related issue; conversely, roughly 20 percent of the general youth populace have such an issue. As indicated by a general supposition survey concentrating on juvenile delinquency and maladjustment, a dominant part of individuals surveyed saw distinct options for imprisonment -, for example, group emotional wellness treatment, tutoring, and professional preparing - as powerful approaches to restore adolescents. Moreover, 8 out of 10 surveyed unequivocally supported taking ceaselessly a percentage of the cash states spend on imprisoning youth guilty parties and utilizing that financing to pay for directing, instruction, and occupation preparing.

Juvenile Justice and Delinquency Prevention Act

Because of far reaching misuses in state and nearby juvenile equity offices, Congress passed the Juvenile Justice and Delinquency Prevention Act in 1974. The JJDPA serves as the essential government subsidizing stream for juvenile equity administrations to states and regions that deliberately credit to its center necessities. Among different necessities, the JJDPA set up guidelines to guarantee that juveniles who submit minor or "status offenses" are not held in secure control, shield juveniles from being detained in grown-up correctional facilities or lock-ups for amplified times of time, address the unbalanced contact adolescents of shading have with the juvenile equity continuum, and different insurances. Through these center prerequisites, the JJDPA is intended to encourage administrations and backings to avert juvenile delinquency and, in cases in which young people enter the juvenile equity framework, insurances to guarantee that they are not unduly presented to mischief or injury while detained.

As per a 2008 overview of the states directed by the Coalition for Juvenile Justice, 55 of 56 states and regions deliberately partake in the JJDPA and 85 percent are consistent with all JJDPA center prerequisites. One of the genuine advantages of the JJDPA is the government/state association it makes through the U.S. Office of Juvenile Justice and Delinquency Prevention; thus, states and regions incredibly esteem the chance to get specialized help and offer effective practices with one another and the OJJDP. Through little interests in effective projects, the central government has the capacity offer the open door for states and domains to repeat fruitful projects, the aftereffect of which is would have liked to be a general change in the way juvenile equity frameworks react to adolescents' remarkable needs.

In spite of the fact that the standards of the JJDPA are commendable and have made key securities for adolescents, usage difficulties hold on - subsidizing confinements, absence of fitting staffing and preparing, and different difficulties keep the acknowledgment of the first vision of the JJDPA.

Reauthorization

Promoters of mental medicinal services view reauthorization of the JJDPA as a chance to address these difficulties. The Juvenile Justice and Delinquency Prevention Act was most as of late reauthorized in 2004, and endeavors are in progress to reauthorize the demonstration in the 111th Congress. Subsequent to being presented in the Senate, the Juvenile Justice and Delinquency Prevention Reauthorization Act (S. 678) was endorsed by the Senate Judiciary Committee, subsequently sending the bill to the Senate floor for thought. Despite the fact that a friendly bill has yet to be presented in the House of Representatives, endeavors are in progress to push for Senate entry in 2010 to reinforce endeavors in the House.

Among a few enhancements, S. 678 makes imperative moves to fortify the capacity of state and regional juvenile equity frameworks to meet the substance use and psychological well-being necessities of young people by fusing the accompanying:

New motivators for enhancing psychological wellness and fixation issue screenings, treatment, preoccupation, and re-passage administrations.

An increment of government approvals for center juvenile equity programs.

Reinforcements of the relationship in the middle of OJJDP and taking part states and domains to encourage expanded agreeability with the center prerequisites of the JJDPA.

To accomplish reauthorization of the JJDPA in 2010, a variety of support associations are taking part in a national coalition exertion. Through this coalition, juvenile equity, child welfare and youth advancement associations show a bound together message in backing of improving the JJDPA.

Adolescents who perpetrate unlawful acts frequently confront a difficult task to enhance their lives, and it is our employment as group suppliers, promoters, and individuals from our groups to guide them in a way that shields them from risk and gives them the chance to accomplish more. In spite of the fact that reauthorization of the JJDPA won't resolve all difficulties in serving equity included young people, it will absolutely get us closer.

Juvenile Crime: Don't Let One Mistake Damage the Life of Your Child

As indicated by the Office of Juvenile Justice and Delinquency Prevention (OJJDP), delinquency case rates for the most part increment with the age of the juvenile. In 2008, U.S. law authorization offices captured more or less 2.11 million adolescents less than 18 years old. Lamentably, the issue of juvenile delinquency is turning out to be more confused and numerous wrongdoing aversion programs either don't exist or are unequipped to manage the issue. Also, as more concerns are raised about youth roughness, a more prominent number of immature guilty parties are being taken care of in the grown-up criminal equity framework. On the off chance that your child has been accused of a juvenile wrongdoing, your first step ought to be to contact a qualified juvenile safeguard lawyer to guarantee your child's rights are secured.

Juveniles versus Grown-up Offenders

The United States does not have an all inclusive juvenile equity framework; the laws separating in the middle of juvenile and grown-up wrongdoers contrast state-by-state. The fundamental distinction between the treatment of juvenile and grown-up wrongdoers is that the juvenile court framework concentrates principally on treatment and recovery, while grown-up criminal courts are predicated on discipline. Then again, in more genuine cases, a juvenile may be exchanged to grown-up criminal court and attempted as a grown-up, contingent upon the age of the wrongdoer, irritating history, and the seriousness of the offense. Albeit numerous states demonstrate a base age for exchange averaging somewhere around ten and fifteen years of age, about 50% of U.S. states don't indicate a base age. In a few states, there are statutory rejection laws set up which direct particular offenses for which indictment as a grown-up is obligatory. Moreover, as of January 2010, two U.S. states arraign every one of the 16- and 17-year-old juvenile guilty parties as grown-ups.

Juvenile Delinquent Offenders

There are various circumstances managing whether an energetic guilty party will be attempted in juvenile court or grown-up criminal court, a hefty portion of which differ contingent upon the state. In the event that the arraignment accuses a more seasoned juvenile of an especially genuine or vicious offense, the indicting lawyer may ask for that the juvenile be attempted as a grown-up. A wrongdoer matured fifteen, sixteen or seventeen, for instance, may be attempted as a grown-up in the event that they are accused of a brutal wrongdoing like ambush, torching or assault. Different cases of law violations which may lead juveniles to be attempted in grown-up criminal court include:

- Brutal Crimes
- Burglary
- Murder
- Weapon's ownership
- Burglary/Theft
- Vandalism
- Auto burglary

- Theft

- Medication and Alcohol Violations

- Drug ownership

- Alcohol law infringement

- Inebriated and messy behavior

- Medication ill-use

- Purpose to offer medications

- Juvenile Status Offenders

There are likewise sure offenses which apply just to juveniles and not to grown-ups, called status offenses. As it were, these demonstrations may be viewed as unlawful when performed by people under a particular age, while staying legitimate for others. Normal status offenses incorporate truancy, fleeing, check in time infringement, hopelessness, and underage liquor utilization.

Juvenile status wrongdoers are recognized from juvenile reprobate guilty parties in that the previous wrongdoers have not carried out a demonstration that would be viewed as a wrongdoing on the off chance that it were conferred by a grown-up, while the recent have.

Lawful Help for Juvenile Offenders

At the point when a minor carries out a wrongdoing, they are regularly attempted and sentenced by a court framework separate from that which tries grown-up wrongdoers. There are likewise separate organizations assigned for juvenile guilty parties, called juvenile confinement focuses. After a juvenile perpetrates a wrongdoing, it is up to the juvenile court to focus the level of danger the juvenile postures to society, and also the advantages acquired via imprisonment in a juvenile confinement focus. Despite the fact that juveniles are ordinarily treated uniquely in contrast to grown-ups when accused of a wrongdoing, regardless they have the same rights. In the event that your child has been accused of a juvenile wrongdoing, it is discriminating that you guarantee your child's rights are ensured. Try not to let one misstep adversely influence whatever remains of your child's life; contact an accomplished juvenile barrier attorney today.

Treating Juvenile Delinquency

Juvenile delinquency or expanded frequencies of law violations submitted by juveniles are a matter of social worry that requires quick consideration from all quarters of society. The best way to lessen juvenile delinquency rates is to comprehend the issue in a more extensive viewpoint as opposed to disciplines or revenge.

One needs to utilize a mixture of approaches to treat juvenile guilty parties. Some of these medications are recorded underneath.

Organic Interventions:

One essential purpose behind juvenile delinquency or brutal conduct in juveniles has been unusual natural conditions and neurological procedures. A few samples incorporate neurophysiologic anomalies and unusual working of steroid hormones and neurotransmitter frameworks. These issues can be dealt with or adjusted by utilizing medications and other pharmacological operators, subsequently decreasing the danger of juvenile delinquency to a certain degree.

Subjective behavioral Approach:

Forceful practices and an improved probability of viciousness in children or teenagers can happen as a consequence of psychological lacks, for example, inadequate critical thinking and useless speculation forms. With a specific end goal to treat such inadequacies, there are two intriguing methodologies that can be received. One methodology includes preparing in social abilities and genius social practices, for example, controlling outrage and showing good values. Another methodology is to create critical thinking aptitudes and expand restraint and social responsively in a person. Multi-systemic Therapy:

This is another promising treatment strategy that has been powerful in decreasing against social conduct among juvenile guilty parties. Multi-systemic treatment is a financially savvy technique that focuses on taking care of various issues that are experienced by a guilty party. These may incorporate family issues, issues in the area, or issues brought on because of companion or in the school. Multi-systemic treatment is perfectly customized treatment approach that addresses particular needs of the patient by giving a situation to enhance participation among relatives and build family relational abilities. Gatherings are likewise directed with a specific end goal to promoter the needs of the pre-adult.

CHAPTER SEVEN:

AUTHORITATIVE PARENTING

GETS RESPECT AND RESULTS

Effective Parenting Styles And Authoritative Parenting

The same number of parents are on the planet, there are an equivalent measure of incapable and viable parenting styles too. Despite the fact that this is the situation, these styles have been isolated into three distinct classes. There are permissive, authoritarian and authoritative parenting styles that individuals utilization to train their children. The last kind is regularly thought to convey the best results for parents who wish to raise charming, all around acted and independent children.

Along these lines of overseeing children grants parents to have a level of control over their children without being excessively controlling. These parents will have a characterized arrangement of rules laid out and children will be relied upon to take after these rules. Despite the fact that the rules are characterized, they do take into account a certain level of adaptability.

These parents have the capacity to express their adoration for their children and are secure in the information that such warmth does not obscure the lines in the matter of restraining the children. At the point when the children get more seasoned they will be permitted more flexibility and obligation while as yet staying inside of specific parameters of guidelines that have been set down. This is on the premise that at this stage the children can be trusted as they have reacted decidedly to this sort of administration every one of their lives.

Numerous children's health care affiliations are of the feeling that children who have been raised with this administration strategy grow up regarding power and are both socially fruitful and free. A sample of this will be children reacting absolutely to the guideline that while desserts may taste decent they are not by any means that solid.

Authoritarian parenting includes a lot of control by the parents over the children. Numerous vibe that this style is however exorbitantly controlling. Here there are tenets and rules that are inflexible and accordingly take into account no level of adaptability by any means.

Dutifulness is unequivocally accentuated and these parents frequently feel the need to practice control over their children.

These parents don't regularly show their adoration to the children and this can lead the children feeling to some degree rejected. Names are frequently used to depict children's conduct. So if the children don't stick to directions they can be alluded to as being awful. They won't allude to the conduct as being terrible.

The children of this sort of administration framework will either get to be subject to their parents everlastingly or they will oppose their parents and leave home early. As far as the desserts illustration, in these homes desserts would never be considered the children. This administration style can bring more issues that it is worth.

A few individuals lean toward permissive parenting to the above style. Here there is much love demonstrated and children are acknowledged as they seem to be. Parents make not very many requests on their children. This administration style can be defective as children never get the opportunity to discover that there are outcomes to activities. These children are well on the way to be ruined and will oblige spoon bolstering sincerely and physically for the duration of their lives. Of the three parenting styles it does create the impression that authoritative parenting is the best course to go.

Effective Ways of Authoritative Parenting

Be Selective with Battles

Authoritative parenting means picking your fights carefully. Parents who hone authoritative parenting styles realize that their children are not impeccable, and thusly, don't pass judgment on them for their autonomous considerations. Now that it's out in the open, they empower it. This is the reason parents who hone this style must choose what is most imperative to them. This helps them to pick their fights with their children admirably, as opposed to having clashes about each seemingly insignificant detail conceivable.

No Nagging

Parents who give long addresses are thought to be naggers by their children. Inevitably, children figure out how to block their parents out, making this an exceptionally ineffectual system for parenting. Authoritative parents keep their words brief, while making their point solidly. For instance, as opposed to bothering children about cleaning their rooms, attempt this methodology: Calmly tell your children, "Put the majority of your toys in the toy box", or "Overlap up each one of those clean garments and put them away where they have a place."

Set Clear Limits

It's about setting points of confinement and imparting them plainly to your children. It is additionally about being predictable with authorizing those breaking points. Never permit your children to arrange concerning unmistakably comprehended guidelines. For instance, when you drop your little girl off at a gathering, you are clear in the matter of what time you will be lifting her up. No special cases. When you arrive and she can't help disagreeing longer, don't get furious or contend with her. In any case, don't move either. Just advise her in a quiet way, "This is the time we conceded to. Close the entryway. Now is the ideal time to go."

Results and Authoritative Parenting

Some parenting styles are about rebuffing children for negative conduct. Authoritative parenting uses results. Authoritative parents need their children to gain from their mix-ups. This obliges results that are reasonable and sensible. A good sample would be a child who lost their most loved toy subsequent to being advised not to take it outside. An authoritative parenting methodology would be to show compassion for their misfortune, while bringing up the results they are enduring. "I see how agitate you are. Perhaps I can help you think of a few approaches to gain some cash so you can purchase another one."

Authoritative Parenting Rewards

Most child clinicians concur that children hunger for structure. This is one of the parenting styles that furnishes this with strict points of confinement and steady results. Parental desires are high, however the outcomes are wonderful on the grounds that the children acknowledge being treated with affection and appreciation.

This style is thought to be the best of the essential parenting styles.

Authoritative vs. Authoritarian or Permissive Parents

The media have as of late highlighted a key open deliberation among parenting specialists: To be a military authoritarian or an empathic audience? To punish or not to hit? To rebuff or to instruct?

In over two decades as a guardian teacher, I immovably accept that viable control means setting firm breaking points while, in the meantime, approaching children with deference and respect. This is authoritative, not correctional, parenting. What's the distinction?

Illustration: Your children are quarreling over which TV show to watch. The authoritarian guardian cries, "Stop! No more TV for a week! That'll show you children to get along." This guardian directs her answer, and the children have no chance to take care they could call their own issues or figure out how to coordinate. They may be angry however are excessively dreadful, making it impossible to express their actual sentiments.

The authoritative guardian says in quiet, clear voice, "In the event that both of you can work out an approach to share your TV time, the pleasure is all mine to watch. If not, the TV goes off." These guardian uses firms teach (expressing a result that will come about if the quarreling proceeds), additionally controls children deferentially toward working out their own answer -and afterward finishes. In the event that she doesn't complete, she is not a sound guardian and her announcement turns into a void danger that her children won't consider important.

The issue with the authoritarian ("Do it in light of the fact that I say as much!") approach is that it utilizes grown-up muscle to compel adolescents to comply. This may work in the short run. Be that as it may, over the long haul, children may turn out to be more resistant and rebellious. Some may get to be tricky and do likewise again yet are less rushed not to get got. A child who's always under a guardian's thumb will discover approaches to dodge or keep away from the principles.

Here are a few tips to help you turn into a more viable guardian without turning into a sucker or a tyrant:

- Pick your fights. Parents and children have clashing needs. Grown-ups need to rush. Children need to dally. We need some request. They like to make messes. Conflicts are inescapable, however don't get maneuvered into each encounter. One of my most loved sayings is "In case you're not specific, you're not compelling." Decide what's truly essential to you, such as going out on time in the morning without shouting or fits - yours or theirs. Converse with children around evening time about how to get prepared on time the following morning. (Case in point: Set out garments together and makes snacks that night, or have a check rundown of what should be done to abstain from "morning franticness." This way you'll all start the day on a more satisfied note.)

- Talk less. Children get to be "parent hard of hearing" when we interminably address, bother, order, scrutinize, and wheedle. They've heard it all sometime recently, so they block us out. To get children to tune in, the trap is to abbreviate the message. Quickness is power. As opposed to lecturing about how untidy their rooms are, make a brief indifferent remark that depicts what should be done: "Those filthy garments have a place in the hamper" or "Books go on the rack."

- Set clear, firm breaking points. Illustration: Before your child goes to a companion's home, tell him precisely what time he must return home. On the off chance that you touch base to lift him up and he tends to disagree longer, you can say, "I know you're having a good time, yet its six o'clock." If he opposes, don't be conflicted by saying, "Alright, only five more minutes." Don't contend. Just express, "Six o'clock was our understanding. We have to go now."

- Use results rather than discipline. Sample: Your child leaves his new roller sharpened pieces of steels outside overnight after you've reminded him to bring them inside. They're stolen. An authoritarian guardian would address: "I cautioned you, however you never hear me out. You got exactly what you merited! That is the last time I'll purchase you anything costly."

That won't show him to be less reckless with his things. It will just make him irate, uncouth, or angry toward you. Rather, you could take an authoritative: "I can see you're disturb that your roller edges are gone and that you'll need to manage without them. Perhaps you can think about an approach to gain some cash toward another pair." An empathic reaction like this one shows a lesson in obligation without being corrective.

- Express your indignation without affront. It's just human to get upset when children defy or incite us. Parents have a privilege to feel furious, however we don't have any privilege to hurt, affront, disparage, or startle children.

In case you're going to blast, take a "grown-up time-out" to chill. You could say, "I'll be in my space for 10 minutes, and we'll talk about this when I turn out." Parents who utilization belittling dialect or lash out physically neglect to show regard in light of the fact that they're being insolent toward the child. This doesn't help a child build up a still, small voice, and beating models the very conduct that we need children to keep away from.

Admiration is a two-way road: Kids learn it best on the off chance that we demonstrate it. They won't figure out how to regard themselves or others if appreciation has not been given to them. Another approach to show admiration is to listen to your child, particularly when he is upset. Listening nearly - without interfering with or infusing grown-up answers - demonstrates to you are truly intrigued and think about him.

Despite the fact that they don't generally demonstrate to it and likely won't thank you right then and there, children truly do need parents to give protected, unsurprising structure in their lives. We can do that by being an authoritative guardian who sets confines on conduct, additionally treats kids the way we all need to be dealt with - with adoration, poise and appreciation.

CHAPTER EIGHT: ADHD LESSONS FOR PARENTS: I HAVE BEEN THERE

ADHD Information For Parents - Latest News and Experiments

In the immense dash to see all the more about ADHD issue, various fascinating truths have risen which ought to help us to comprehend our way to deal with ADHD treatment. It ought to additionally help us in treating ADHD data with the suspicion/regard it merits.

Supernatural Meditation ?

Transcendental contemplation (TM) has hit the ADHD features. Specialists at the George Washington University concentrated on a gathering of center school understudies who were taught how to do TM for only ten minutes twice per day. All the children had more prominent or lesser ADHD issues and after the investigation was over, there was a 50% decrease in ADHD side effects and the children had the capacity think better, had less behavioral issues and were a great deal less hyperactive.. More examinations will should be done before we send our children to TM lessons however it is a promising improvement in that it could decrease the quantity of ADHD children on psychotics/psycho stimulants.

Understudies Abusing ADHD Drugs

The quantity of understudies utilizing ADHD medications to power their recollections and focus has never been higher (5%) as per a study which included three noteworthy US colleges. These were Duke, Michigan and North Carolina. Of the 3,000 understudies met, the dominant part were satisfied with the outcomes and not in the slightest degree stressed over medication reliance, sleep deprivation or dietary problems. Yet these are the same symptoms that ADHD children need to adapt to when endorsed these medications. The three most prominent medications utilized by the understudies were Ritalin , Concerta and Adderall. The possibility of our childhood being for all time on brain modifying psycho stimulants for all their life is disturbing no doubt!

Jamie Oliver's Campaign

In the UK, the level headed discussion on corpulence and hyperactivity in children has been taken up by the exceptionally prevalent TV culinary specialist/master Jamie Oliver. He loves the thought of Scottish schools giving free adjusted suppers to children in the initial three years of elementary school yet is most worried that the duties paid by meeting expectations mothers is not being put resources into giving cookery lessons to children which would ingrain in them a familiarity with nourishment from an early age. He needs a £6 billion interest in school suppers and cookery lessons. The British Heart Foundation is worried about the false claims utilized by nourishment producers as a part of promoting kids' sustenances - they never say certainties, for example, high sugar, salt and fat substance, also perilous sustenance colorings - the recent have been connected to ADHD manifestations.

Media Exposure And ADHD ?

In the USA, the National Institutes of Health and Yale University have examined all the studies done on media presentation and their impacts on kids' wellbeing. The studies/examination secured such ranges as, TV, feature, PC, the Web. It is awful news and the children who are overexposed to some or all these media are prone to wind up with a portion of the accompanying issues:- weight, medication misuse, liquor ill-use, smoking, untimely sexual movement , hyperactivity and ADHD.

Is it conceivable that there is a dependable site where you can discover some data on ADHD elective treatment and ADHD regular cures? More concerned parents are turning out to be more careful about routine ADHD drug and the pill-popping society which as we have seen above can prompt issues proceeding into pre-adulthood and past. Time to shrewd up and the connection beneath will kick you off all in all correct.

Top Ten Tips for Parenting ADHD and Spirited Kids

1. Advocate for your child. This implies you have to "turn" your child's conduct to companions, family and educators. Has your child's jokes been any more

regrettable than our driving government officials? Likely not. Envision the spinmeisters on syndicated programs who attempt to get their legislators chose. Do likewise for your child.

2. Mentor your child to name and feel OK with every one of their feelings. Children act awful when they are distraught, dismal or "terrified". When you mentor your child to let you know what she feels, her awful conduct will recuperate.

3. Glimpse inside yourself. Infrequently children carry on unexpressed clashes of their parents. Is it accurate to say that you are battling with melancholy, uneasiness, and wrath? Get help for yourself and your children will take care of business.

4. Consider yourself a mentor. Your occupation is to mentor your child to accomplishment in social, passionate and instructive settings. Now and then the answer is practice, practice, rehearse. Try not to get demoralized in the event that you need to rehash yourself again and again.

5. Ask yourself: "If my child's most disappointing conduct was intended to show me something, what might it be?" Many parents discover themselves half troubled and half awed at their child's lack of interest to individuals satisfying. Once in a while this is only the lesson parents need to learn in their own lives - numerous parents have get to be

imbalanced in going to an excessive amount to looking for endorsement from others.

6. Disregard the opposition. Your child can at present endeavor to be exceptional without it being about correlations to other children. ADHD and vivacious children are touchy to pressure created by parents' aggressiveness and the apprehension based inspiration hinders them.

7. Keep Yourself Alive! It takes a considerable measure of vitality to stay aware of ADHD and energetic children. You have to turn into your own particular vitality source. Nourish your own particular interests. On the off chance that

you are hitched, work to expand your closeness with your accomplice. In the event that you are single, keep your own particular affection life alive.

8. Honor the bit of confidence in all demonstrations of disobedience. Each time your child doesn't do what you requesting that they do, approach them for a clarification. Honor their free thinking and consider what a piece of it you may need to fuse into your control. Keep on demanding that your child regard your standards while exhibiting admiration for their own cadence and rationale.

9. Hone safeguard prescription. Commonly children's terrible conduct is a confused

endeavor to get a few valuable consideration. Fuel your child up with the most elevated octane vitality you can at a young hour in the day. Spend a couple of minutes being altogether present with your child. Look at them without flinching, touch them affectionately and listen nearly to your child. This extreme vicinity will give them what they need and take off edgy supplications for consideration. In some cases only a couple of minutes will counteract extensive vitality depleting bothers.

10. Associate with your child's educator. Examination has demonstrated over numerous decades that your child's instructive results are firmly connected

with how much the educator enjoys your child and the amount they anticipate from your child. This is the reason you have to backer for your child in the meantime as you unite with your child's educator. Show huge appreciation for your child's instructors and attempt to produce a nearby partnership with him or her. They will go the additional mile for your child.

What we Learned in Kindergarten

In preschool, where a major lump of the educational program rotates around friendliness, you can hear the particular subtle elements of a social conduct weaving through the everyday dialog. Listen to the instructor: "Sit in your spot and put your hands in your lap. Hold up until the ball is in your court to talk. Raise your hand to say something." Keep to the calendar: "Now is the right time to stop what you are doing. Get the toys. Put them conveniently in their spots on the rack. At that point come sit discreetly on the floor covering." There you have the plainly enunciated, effectively imagined miniaturized scale steps that instruct preschoolers to mingle, arrange and "act" in a gathering setting. At that point as scholastics move to the front of classroom needs, social educational module blurs.

For our testing friends and family, who keep on expecting to hear the data imbedded in those smaller scale steps, school is a puzzling and hostile spot. The understudy with Asperger Syndrome who loves to be the scientist of the truths for a science undertaking is uninformed of the obliged 'give and take' in a helpful learning gathering. Since she appears to be oppressive and resolute, her associates block her out, prohibit her from gathering enrollment, and she has missed out on the delights of learning. The shrewd, dynamic ADHD child has no methods to contain his motivations and channel his plentiful vitality into his schoolwork, thus meanders around on the fringe of the learning activity however he would truly love to be middle of everyone's attention with his gifts.

Alongside their "testing" attributes, each one of our testing friends and family have their interesting and frequently extremely enchanting arrangement of qualities, abilities and premiums, which they long to impart to others somehow. Be that as it may, their practices have a tendency to send an alternate, conflicting, self-subverting message. She may be exclusively centered around a distraction or her compulsiveness. He may be a dug in avoider, a self-named supervisor, or a full time worrier- - or maybe he doesn't appear to stress at all over the results of his decisions. Her super affectability to touch or sound may welcome distance. Center and senior high children are marked "washouts" on the grounds that they are seen fumblingly meandering, lost in the lobbies they could call their own schools.

These are cases of the child sorts who are stuck inside themselves, with their countenances squeezed upon the windows that post at the social universe of their associates, to whom everything appears to come easily. Their companions know how to fit in and their prize is acknowledgement. What's more, these testing children grow up to be grown-ups that additionally meander -lost seeing someone, work settings and their social group. They are stuck in a befuddling, secluding spot, and for the most part misconstrued, misread, secrets to themselves as well as other people. Furthermore, what they are truly imparting through their conduct, is the way extremely troublesome it is to adjust to their general surroundings.

The Hidden Curriculum

What stands between the individuals who are in the activity and those stuck within watching out? It has get to be known as the 'shrouded educational program.' They need relentless training and particular ability honing through those small scale steps on the grounds that it is not programmed for them to "get" what is going on and afterward make sense of 'what happened' or 'take in their lessons' from playing unreasonable or breaking guarantees, or "hoarding" the scene. In his book, It's So Much Work to Be Your Friend, Richard Lavoie, M.A. M.Ed., talks about how every school has it claim individual society, which decides the subtle elements of the concealed educational module and subsequently what it takes to be "in." He says "Your child is tried on his scholarly abilities at regular intervals, yet his social associations are "tried" and assessed several times every day."

For our testing friends and family who may have a conclusion of ADHD, High Functioning Autism or Asperger Syndrome or another that carries with it behavioral difficulties, the tenets of social acknowledgement are undetectable ...until they have the chance to take in the miniaturized scale steps.

What is a Micro Step?

'Miniaturized scale steps' are the extremely little most modest instructional steps that give the most particular and direct data to help your testing cherished one take in the how-to's of being social or taking care of business. Miniaturized scale steps are the missing fixings that lie between what parents and instructors think about conduct change, and what is left to embed into their conduct change or social expertise building system. Recognizing those key smaller scale steps can be an exceptionally difficult riddle. Miniaturized scale ability building is an inventive and deliberate procedure where little clumps of aptitudes are woven together, with the unbelievably grand result of showing our testing friends and family to explore life autonomously, suitably and cheerfully!

The Broad Stroke Skill Sets

Taking after are a percentage of the more extensive gatherings of abilities which separate into the smaller scale steps that are vital to class and social achievement:

1) mindfulness and self reflection

2) fellowship building

3) open suitability

4) non verbal signs and passionate messages

5) thought: giving it and getting it

6) decision and choice making

7) inclination instruments and quieting procedures

8) giving individual qualities and intrigues something to do

9) dissatisfaction and strength

10) taking care of dismissal and harassing

CHAPTER NINE: PARENTING FROM THE HEART

At the point when mothering from the heart, you feel so much empathy and adoration for your child. Despite the fact that teach and redress is a piece of your numerous parts, it once in a while may bring inconvenience due to the affection in your heart for your child. One thing as Mothers we should never forget, what we put into our child is definitely what will leave them. Galatians 6:9.

Is regular going to be smooth and simple? Is ordinary going to be without difficulties and meetings? It unquestionably isn't. At the point when Mothering from the heart, your endeavors will be compensated by God. As we keep on imploring, look for God for astuteness and comprehension, we will feel awesome achievement in our journey as a Mother.

Mothering from the heart ought to be a characteristic affair, so common that we will do whatever it takes to demonstrate our children we mind and have much love for them. At the point when Mothering from the heart you look for no paybacks, your actual commute is to be fruitful in what you do. Mothering from the heart is a unique assignment that we all appear to make it through. Our prizes will indicate in the natural product our children produce, and we will be so pleased with what we have done.

We can recall the times when we needed to simply quit and say "Am I a good Mother?" As we keep on growing and seek after our journey as a Mother, we live up to expectations it all, for the straightforward truth - we are similar to no other!

Also, a few specialists accept there is no better type of correspondence with regards to parenting than NVC (peaceful correspondence). This article covers the rudiments of NVC and gives accommodating tips on the best way to apply it in your family home.

Exactly what is NVC?

NVC remains for peaceful correspondence and the premise of it is that individuals can hear one out another with sympathy and empathy and without judgment of feedback. This type of correspondence stems from truly needing to regard the needs and sentiments of all relatives.

Illustration of ordinary NVC

A standard circumstance in numerous families with little children is that things get muddled. Envision now that it's the end of a taxing day mother still has a million things to do before putting the children to bed. She strolls into the kid's rooms and is welcomed with colored pencils on the floor, paper all around, toys, Lego and a plain old chaos.

In the typical situation it would be simple, and naturally thus, for mother to get surprise and vent. She may say things like, "this room is a pigsty and it makes me so irate!," "how on the planet did this get so chaotic? I just can't stand it any longer" and "we're not going to bed until this room is spotless!" Mom will get exceptionally focused on and may even yell and look extremely irate.

Presently take the same situation however apply NVC. For this situation mother would take a full breath at the site of the room. At that point she would let herself know, "the room is muddled however it's not the apocalypse" or "there are a couple colored pencils, papers and toys on the take after yet this can be immediately cleaned away and we can go ahead with our night."

NVC helps you place circumstances into point of view on the grounds that let's be honest rooms get muddled and it's not the apocalypse, but rather in light of the fact that so large portions of us are worried by advanced life its anything but difficult to lose our cool at the site of an untidy room. NVC helps you defeat these feelings and place everything into a superior viewpoint.

Interfacing through NVC

Utilizing NVC as a part of ordinary life will actually help you bond and fabricate shared regard in the middle of you and your child. It doesn't, then again, imply that children can do whatever they like however that essentially you consider every circumstance and attempt to comprehend why your child responds the way they do.

For instance on the off chance that you ask a child "would you be able to please secure the colored pencils and papers now so we can have time for a sleep time story" will generally be met with a more pleasing answer than if you hollered at your child "clean this room up now or there is no story today!"

Parenting from the heart is a holy and compensating trip. You can set up a more elevated amount of association with your children through the festival and investigation of your heart relationship. At the point when our own soul perceives the inside shine of our children, we can use this bond for carrying on with an existence of peace, love, and equalization. These nine components are intended to be the philosophical beginning stage for you to see all existence with more prominent centrality and start to parent from the heart.

- Honor: Living an existence of honor is to exhibit truth, trustworthiness, and uprightness in your activities and convictions. We frequently identify with the idea of honor when making a promise to our nation or taking a marital pledge, yet do we consider regarding our spirit's way every last day? Permit your decisions and conduct to mirror the best parts of you furthermore assume liability when your activities influence another. At the point when living with incredible admiration of each spirit, you start to see the world as an astounding chance to share love. Perceiving and respecting the light inside of others permits a closeness and respect past common experience and boundlessly advantages our families.

- Empathy: The capacity to feel, sense, or identify with the encounters of another. Realizing what it is similar to stroll in their shoes or wear their cap, as it were. Having comprehension and empathy for the activities and practices of those we experience implants us with a profound feeling of connectedness. We exhibit a higher mindfulness when we desert cruel judgments and select rather to understand others. Our children are better served when we can affectionately unite with their vitality mark and attempt to see from their remarkable point of view. Permit your heart to lead the path to an existence of sweet comprehension.

- Altruism: The idea of unselfishness is carrying on with an existence in advantage of the hobbies of others-being of administration to society and the world without increase to the self. This is an establishment confidence in a horde of religions, for example, Christianity,

Buddhism, and Judaism. Consider philanthropy being pleasant and kind to people around you without respect to a result for yourself. It is not being a hireling to somebody or affected by another's control. Showing this conduct to our children is the most ideal approach to sustain their inner feeling of kindheartedness and liberality.

- Resonance: Our fiery association with somebody or something, when we are in agreement with another, tuned into and influenced by the same recurrence, vibration, or wavelength. Regarding and supporting our vivacious associations is the following supernatural stride in parenting. Being aware you could call your own vitality signature and delicate to your child's engages a family to carry on with a dynamic life in splendid natural concordance. Envision what your family will have the capacity to do when you cultivate reverberation in your home. There is no restriction to what can be, as adoration knows no limits.

- Trust: When we talk about trust, we are alluding to dependence on a conviction. Having confidence and conviction in somebody or something. At the point when carrying on with a heart-focused life, you have to depend on yourself, as well as in the astounding conceivable outcomes inborn in the Universe. We are going far from limits and permitting God's beauty to take a higher part in our lives. Know with sureness that whatever is happening in your reality from minute to minute is by Divine outline. Trust your children and they will believe you.

- Gratitude: The feeling and vitality we radiate when in profound energy about the circumstances in our reality. Since a long time ago held onto as a crucial ideals in logic and innumerable religions, appreciation prompts an existence of peace, wellbeing, and thriving. Being appreciative for the differing encounters of living specifically corresponds to accomplishment in accomplishment, prosperity, and social holding. Notwithstanding your family's difficulties or favors, ingraining a feeling of appreciation for the supernatural occurrence of life itself raises your vivacious vibration, encouraging reverberation in your souls. Be thankful for what is and experience the marvel of Heaven on Earth.

- Love: The Divine Spirit is the sign and wellspring of all adoration in the Universe, grandly communicating in the grin of a child, a butterfly on the breeze, and the grandness of a mountain range. We every are innovative articulations of adoration. Illustrating, supporting, and praising affection is the importance and motivation behind all life. It is a decision to permit our cherishing light to radiate through our activities, goals, and connections. Do we decide to radiate beauty and to carry on with an existence of adoration? Permit the astounding imaginative power of adoration to change your reality from a dreadful battle to a heart-shining, serene presence.

- Opportunity: Our opportunity to make utilization of the circumstances throughout our life. We regularly identify with this idea just in positive encounters, for example, an offer of work or being chosen to get a grant. It is, on the other hand, a lot more. Our regular conditions and events, even circumstances we regard as negative, are open doors for development and edification. We pick regardless of whether to exploit what precedes us, the old saying of making lemonade from harsh lemons. The flexibility and chance to grow our observations and carry on with another existence of heart-based parenting is our own, in the event that we decide to grab the day.

- Wellness: Making a pledge to health is pivotal when incorporating instinctive parenting strategies. We must have a sound admiration of our bodies, psyches, and spirits, knowing our whole being is an instrument. Regardless of the possibility that we live with perpetual sickness or handicap, we are consummate and precisely as Spirit proposed. You can grasp prosperity by showing legitimate consideration. Be aware of what you eat, how you move, and the measure of rest you get. Require some serious energy to process your feelings and discharge any antagonism caught in your body. The wonderful sanctuary of you will admire your gave motion. Adoring tend to your child is improved when you additionally nurture yourself.

CHAPTER TEN: CONCLUSION: THE VERDICT OF TIGER PARENTING

Suicidal Ideation

In spite of the fact that suicide is a genuinely substantial subject and evokes a wide range of negative pictures, all things considered it ought to be discussed, especially what causes suicidal ideation in children and how to deal with such a scenario.

At the point when choosing what angles to cover with this subject, and there are numerous, I chose to discuss hazard evaluation. A standout amongst the most imperative parts of my employment while working with high hazard customers was knowing acceptable behavior quick notwithstanding suicidal ideations.

On the off chance that a child you know is communicating suicidal contemplations, these must be considered important at all times. There are a couple issues that you ought to be mindful of, and figure out the responses to, so as to decide how inescapable suicidal expectation is. To begin with, figure out whether the child has an arrangement to confer suicide. This will give an evidence on the off chance that they find themselves able to finish a suicide endeavor. Besides, figure out whether the child has the methods in which to complete a suicide. On the off chance that the child is looking at slaughtering themselves with an overdose, do they have the pills, medications, liquor or mix of these to complete the arrangement? Thirdly, figure out whether the child has the lethality to succeed with the suicide. This implies that if the child does to be sure have the pills, medications, liquor or mix of those important to complete the overdose, will it be deadly? In the event that you don't know without a doubt then accept that it can be deadly.

Thus, for instance, if the child says that they will overdose when everybody is far from the house, then that would be an arrangement. In the event that they say that they have pills, medications and liquor available to them, or access to them, then this says that they have the intends to do it. On the off chance that the kind of pills, sort of medications and measure of liquor is sufficient to execute them then they without a doubt have the lethality to succeed in the suicide endeavor. Regardless of the possibility that they don't have the lethality to complete a suicide, for instance, they have a little measure of hormone pills, a few joints and a half liter of wine, then this may not be deadly but rather by the by they ought to still be alluded to a specialist or family specialist for appraisal of melancholy or suicidal ideation.

Unless you have particular preparing in figuring out whether any pills, medications, liquor or blend of them can be deadly, then I would firmly ask you to call a specialist or 911 and have the individual gotten for an evaluation. The simple recommendation of suicide is a genuine sign that a man has more profound issues that need treatment. Kindly don't put off suicidal ideations as something that may be excessively humiliating, making it impossible to manage, or that you don't believe is not sufficiently kidding to warrant getting help with. Notwithstanding on the off chance that a child has communicated suicidal contemplations in the past and has never completed, or has communicated them as a piece of "carrying on", don't expect that this time will be the same. Numerous individuals express suicidal ideations various times before they proceed with it.

You can call any drug store, doctor's facility, specialist's office or medication treatment focus for data on the lethality of any mix of medications or liquor, and also for direction about what to do in the event that you are uncertain. In any case, ACT, you may spare an existence.

The response to the draw of suicide, to the suicidal ideation, to the dream of "freedom" through death and "penance" through self-assault, can just get through the Light. In a few ways, suicidal ideation is the passing itself and the main response to this internal demise is not the physical demise, but rather the Life, the True Life and Eternal Life. The breath of Life that can free the suicidal personality must be given by God, when called upon. Whether it gets through an accommodating word from someone else, an occasion that makes us see things in an unexpected way, or restorative help (yes, God meets expectations through specialists as well), the answer is constantly through the wellspring of Life and that is God. Our calls upon the Highest Forces of Light are constantly listened.

Jesus is a standout amongst the most intense strengths for Life and Truth and calling upon Him (whether we have faith in Him or not) can't but rather delineate the darkest murkiness -on the off chance that we let Him. This is imperative to do, when enticed by suicidal ideation, for four reasons:

1)Because, as effectively said, God is the Source of Life and just the genuine Source of Life can disperse the dim surrender all expectations regarding passing musings.

2) Because God doesn't pass judgment. Dissimilar to His religious (self-designated) human delegates on Earth, who frequently are extremely judgmental about suicide, God's adoration is absolutely genuine and unshaken by any considerations or sentiments, however edgy

they may be. He is dependably, always gushing that interminable waterway of affection, sympathy, tending to us, regardless of what state we may be in. An in number calculate suicidal ideation is frequently the blame about having fizzled, even blame about being in this state, which then encourages into an endless loop. God does not get at all put off by our state. He is extremely merciful, however not disturb: our darkest musings can't frighten Him away. He can deal with it and He can deal with us. He has all out confidence in us, regardless of how hard we attempt to demonstrate to Him (and ourselves) that we are an acts of futility, to be over with. He knows not. You could say that His affection is blind, all things considered it is precisely the inverse: it is on account of He can see every bit of relevant information about us, past the darkness that obstructs our vision that His adoration is so steady and unchangeable. We can request that he help us see ourselves as He sees us (HE, not his religious human delegates). This can lift the dark smoke of suicidal ideation, as quite a bit of it is about self-assault. Debilitating individuals with damnation in the event that they confer suicide (as a few religions do) is not going to dissuade them from doing as such. It may deflect them from looking for assistance from God (partner Him with the undermining religion) and along these lines push them promote into the sorrow chasm. The best approach to hinder individuals from suicide is to reveal to them the vastness of Love and Light that is as of now there for them. The negative can't be battled with another negative. Yet, just with what is truly positive and this can just originate from Spirit.

3) The third reason we have to call upon the Light, if in this state, is psychic assurance. Sometimes, negative energies get pulled in to the discouraged personality and once in a while (not generally, but rather in some cases) the voice (or thought) that says "Go kill yourself" is not really our own. This need not panic us, on the grounds that God is significantly more capable than any of these elements, and calling upon Jesus, specifically, to secure us and break up the assaulting contemplations can be greatly powerful. The image of the Holy Cross, calling upon Jesus' name, holding His symbol, saying the Lord's Prayer, all these are intense fast approaches to bring security upon us. In Him,

there is nothing to trepidation. The issue is that numerous individuals just don't call upon God for help, regularly on the grounds that they don't have confidence in Him, or these "psychic" things. That is precisely what these energies need, so they can go ahead about their business. Regardless of the fact that you don't trust in them, call upon God to ensure you. That'll do.

4) The fourth motivation behind why we have to call upon God amid the depressive or suicidal time is that in Him lies our actual personality, protected and unscathed. At times, suicidal contemplations come as an aftereffect of our feeling of personality being broken, on account of life circumstances. I see this a great deal in my nation: men who all of a sudden lose their occupation and effects and accordingly, their

accomplice (frequently taking the children along) have their personality (at any rate as it is organized in our Western progress) completely taken to pieces. As the feeling of self goes, alongside the life circumstances, the individual may be enticed to react to the obvious disintegration with physical disintegration. The intuitive thought may be: "In the event that I have nothing, then I am no one, along these lines I would do well to be dead". Yet, the disintegration can be a defining moment for genuine freedom, though in a greatly excruciating way. Whatever the change, however synergist, God keeps our actual personality set up, entire and in place. We can call upon Him, and by calling upon Him, we recollect who we really are and afterward, we feel invigorated. By feeling invigorated, we are freed from the hopelessness. Not by suicide. The genuine personality may not appear to be noteworthy to the outside world. Indeed, the modest holding of the genuine personality (finding the individual we genuinely are and living it) may show up as uneventful, some may even judge it as disappointment. In any case, it is the main accomplishment there is and it is massively intense. It is the particular case that God perceives. Living it and feeling it on the Earth plane is the thing that satisfies God and makes our main goal here work out as expected. It is the main thing that can really fulfill.

Like despondency, suicidal ideation is firmly connected to self-esteem. Also, since our self is a human self, it is likewise connected to human-worth. In numerous spots on the planet, including our Western civilization, people are essentially not esteemed. Some piece of the purpose behind the suicide pandemic in the emergency hit nations, as Greece, is unequivocally this message, inalienable in our cash driven society: "Without cash, you are nothing". I am compelled to admit this message of uselessness has infiltrated numerous individuals' heart, more than they might want to concede. Mentally they differ obviously, they get irate and defiant at the proposal. In any case, what amount of do they truly esteem themselves by and by, if the framework shows them out of the diversion, keeping in mind the end goal to battle for their lives? Other individuals, who additionally mentally can't help contradicting this announcement, showcase this conviction in any case to the person who lost everything. Numerous in the helping calling, including analysts and self-development masters, may not mull over him, in the event that he doesn't have the cash to pay. Companions and associates, even family, quit calling the person who's gone bankrupt. The affectation is more broad than we might want to concede, yet once we understand it (to spare us from future dissatisfaction), it doesn't generally touch us, for there is the best esteem provider of all: God. Also, He has officially given us boundless worth, picking us as His children.

This is the thing that we are. We are not a collection of haphazardly chosen DNA and particles that simply happened to adjust in the right way, a disintegrate of dirt in an indifferent Universe administered just by laws of material science. The Universe is not administered by the laws of physical science, they are being broken all the time by the Will of God! There is another law that guidelines this Universe and it is this one that has permitted the planet and humankind to continue for so long, without blowing separated from the zillions of reasons that could have put it out of parity. The Author of this Law has picked us as His Children. We are not various a ledger or a word after "Occupation". We don't need to demonstrate our value to anybody, not even ourselves. It has been given by Him as of now and that doesn't change. Furnished with this value, it is similar to intersection the ocean of existence with the most mechanically progressed, solid and strong boat: nothing can touch it and even tempests can be knowledgeable about straightforwardness, even maybe with energy. Without the attention to this value, it is similar to swimming with uncovered hands. In the event that a board is given us and the climate is good, sufficiently reasonable. However, in the event that the board (work, compensation, accomplice and so forth.) is taken away and the wind is blowing a bit, we feel like suffocating. Yet our vehicle is right here sitting tight for us, fresh out of the box new and brimming with fuel. It has our name on it. It is for us to cross that ocean with. Why suffocate into it when we can go on it and see it all? Tempests are constantly transient and provincial in any case. The completion of time will dependably come, whatever the trouble.

Suicidal musings are not generally because of money related inconveniences obviously. Matters of adoration -rather, absence of affection are frequently an element in feeling that life is horrendous. Yet, that too is a fantasy, following the forlornness is because of the injury of spiritual detachment, which is dependably the injury underneath human partition. Man left God, however the longing for affection remained. Not knowing how to fulfill it (but rather persistently not wishing to come back to God), Man chose that the wellspring of adoration would now originate from one another, in what the Course in Miracles calls the 'extraordinary relationship'. Scarcely whatever other issue has brought on such a great amount of agony in mankind's heart history than this grave misconception. The horrifying quest for fulfilling human affection is a piece of the motivation behind why a few individuals need to leave life. Once more, the issue here is an aggregate one: other individuals' responses are regularly not supportive, in light of the fact that they too are gotten up to speed in the same deception of void and trepidation. Be that as it may, the individuals who have gotten, esteemed and deliberately acknowledged the life-maintaining thus genuine adoration for God, these ones can help-just by their vicinity. This affection is accessible to all of us and it is not only a hypothetical thought. When you begin uniting with it, it will sustain you more than any sustenance or any human warmth. It won't make any difference on the off chance that others don't comprehend it.

POOR MENTAL HEALTH

5 Ways to Promote Positive Mental Health while still maintaining authority

Positive mental health is an awesome approach to guarantee your children lead a long, glad and healthy life. Keeping up your children's mental health is less demanding than a great many people think and will have a huge effect on your ordinary life.

Might you want to have more vitality? Shouldn't something be said about a pleasant evening rest?

How you might want to go a whole year without getting this season's cold virus once? Accomplishing a positive mental health state won't ensure these things, however it beyond any doubt will offer assistance.

Here are the main 5 things you can do to help advance positive mental health in you and your children:

a) Eating Healthy. Eating fast food 3 times each week and bringing down a couple frosty ones before bed may be simpler than making a home-cooked feast and more pleasant than drinking a chilly glass of water however it won't do a ton for your health. Eating home-cooked sustenance's (particularly leafy foods) and staying far from the fast food joints will help you accomplish the healthy way of life you seek.

b) Drinking Lots of Water. To keep up a healthy way of life, normal people are required to expend no less than eight glasses of water a day. Keeping in mind this appears like it might be a considerable measure, it's really not. Eight glasses is practically proportional to topping off your water restrain a couple times in the middle of waking and going to bed. Keep in mind, in the event that you work out, you will need to expand your water admission to adjust for the water you're blazing off while working out. Drinking water will detoxify your body and restore it back to a healthy state

- particularly in the wake of drinking espresso or hard refreshments.

c) Kick the Bad Habits. We've effectively said it a couple times yet disposing of noteworthy liquor admission will have positive results on your mental health. Moreover, kicking other negative behavior patterns like smoking and drinking extensive measures of espresso will likewise help keep your mental health getting it done.

d) De-Stressing. Anxiety is one of the main sources for poor mental health. When you're worried, your body needs to work harder to keep up and, extra minutes, it will take its toll on your body and your mind. Next time something distressing happens, take a stab at lighting a few candles and scrubbing down. On the off chance that that doesn't work for you, have a go at letting off some steam by heading off to the rec center or going for a run. Keeping a positive outlook will advance positive mental health and kill undue weight on your mind.

e) Booking Regular Check-ups. Shockingly, you can do everything recorded above and still experience the ill effects of mental health issues. Actually, you may have a mental sickness and not even know it. Verify you're mental health is in good condition by occupying general meetings with your specialist. He/she will have the capacity to affirm whether you're way of life is healthy or recognize where you may need to roll out a few improvements.

To sum up, we must understand the way we experience our lives significantly influences everything around us, including our children. Understanding our decisions, practices, musings, feelings, activities, and propensities all intertwine to make our presence, our individual mosaic or embroidered artwork. Our family life is just as solid as the time, adoration, and aim we put toward it. You will procure the fabulous prizes of a heart association with your child in the event that you apply these ideas with commitment into your everyday living. The decision to parent with your heart is yours.

Made in the USA
Las Vegas, NV
11 April 2025

20835555R00187